In Favor of Everything Right

Nyah Peyton

IN FAVOR OF EVERYTHING RIGHT

Cover and Interior Design by Nyah Peyton

Printed by Amazon.com, Inc., in the United States of America.

First printing edition 2020.

ISBN: 978-1-71682-357-2 (paperback)

Amazon.com, Inc.
440 Terry Avenue North
Seattle, WA, 98109

Table of Contents

Introduction

I played soccer for the majority of my life. I started playing when I was four -years -old, and played competitively from the age of 10 to 18 -years old. I planned on playing in college, but decided that I was tired of being a student-athlete, and didn't want to sacrifice the opportunities I would experience being a regular student. I already had to sacrifice so much in middle and high school; I wasn't willing to rob myself of the experience that I wanted in college.

The first time I can remember testing God was when I was about 11 -years -old. There was no tryout for the first club team that I played on. We just took the team we already had and registered as a classic team. However, the following season we had to try out. I was a good player, but not the best. I was strong and athletic, I worked hard, and I was very coachable. My touch on the ball wasn't ideal, I wasn't that fast because I had terrible running form, and I could only use my dominant foot to kick the ball. I was good for my age, but playing classic soccer is a game of a different caliber. Recreational soccer and club soccer are two different worlds. Coming in to the first day of tryouts, I was confident. I knew everyone, and everyone knew me. In my mind, there was no way that I wasn't going to make the team, because I was already on the team!

That confidence dwindled away by the end of the tryout. I did horribly. I was whiffing the ball, missing shots, and making bad passes. My touch was horrible, I was getting outran, I was losing the ball. I mean, it was the whole nine! I looked like I didn't belong there. I felt like I didn't belong there. When my parents came to pick me up, I was dead silent. They asked me how it went, and I said it was okay. As we were pulling out of the parking lot, I looked out of the window toward the fields. I looked up to the sky, and my eyes started watering. I closed them and let the tears run quietly down my face. Then, I started praying.

"God, if You can hear me, please help me. I really want to make the team. I did horribly tonight, and if I don't do better tomorrow night, I won't make it. Help me clean up my touches, help me make the shots, help me keep the ball, help me be strong, give me confidence. I know You can do that for me. Amen."

The innocent prayer of an 11 -year -old girl. I was putting God to the test, having faith that He would show up for me. The next tryout, I prayed again.

"God, remember what I asked for! Please help me tonight. Thank

you in advance. Amen."

I was amazing that evening! Everything I asked for, He granted me. The ride home that evening was much different than the night before. I was all smiles and talked the whole way home about how well I performed and how confident I was about making the team. I remember walking off of the field, thanking God over and over again.

I look back at it now, and I'm in awe of how something so miniscule, could turn into something so great. That day was the day I solidified my faith. That was the day I concluded that prayer works, and that nothing goes unheard, not even the smallest of pleas.

Therapy comes in all shapes and forms. For me, it's poetry and journaling. *In Favor of Everything Right* compiles poems derived from my therapeutic sessions between God and I over the years and the context behind most of the poems in the form of a narrative. The poems with no accompanying narratives, I feel, explain themselves. I'm not a very open person: I'm fearful of being vulnerable. However, through growth and much communion with God, I have realized the power of testimony. This book tackles depression, insecurity, relationships, spirituality, and more. I'm so excited to open my heart and mind to other people who might need some encouragement and reassurance.

This book not only reveals my spiritual journey, but also some of the desires and weaknesses of the flesh, such as gender inequalities, lust, black pride and unity, and normal teenage girl issues regarding boys. Just because I love Jesus doesn't mean that I am immune from regular issues, but I am better-equipped to navigate them in a way that will help me instead of harm me — whether in the moment or in the long run.

God speaks to everyone in different ways. For me, He provides visions, dreams, and physical revelations and events. I can hear Him in my mind. It sounds like a thought that you don't form on your own. It's like you're thinking to yourself, but you don't know what you are going to say. He speaks to me in visions, and He tells me to make the vision plain. This almost always results in artwork. I have painted several visions, some that were intended to be given to others. He speaks to me in my writing. I will feel a tug of the Spirit, and as soon as I begin expressing myself on paper, I don't stop until I am completely empty. These poems and journal entries help me reflect, problem-solve, and get my feelings out of the way in order to make wise choices. He speaks to me through events and physical revelations. He has quite literally saved my life a couple of times, spoken to me directly through the radio, and has answered my prayers right in front of my eyes.

He speaks to me in dreams. When I was sick with viral meningitis in March of 2020, he gave me a dream with a message that I was supposed to pass onto someone who was struggling. I had no idea how to interpret or discern it, and I didn't even try. I just had to relay the message. He gave me another dream prior to that regarding the same individual, and that dream turned into visions and daydreams until I completed the task. God has revealed Himself and all of His glory, power, love, and might to me in many ways. He has never left me, nor forsaken me, even during times when I felt that He did. The key is to listen. You will never hear His voice if you aren't expecting to hear it. When you ask God for guidance, listen for His direction. When you ask God for reassurance, listen to His promises. When you ask God for strength, listen to His affirmations. When you ask God for peace, look for His love and listen to the songs that play in your heart.

This is why I am shameless in my walk. This is why I will blast and sing along to a Kirk Franklin song in a full parking lot. This is why I'm not afraid to admit when I'm wrong. This is why I'm not afraid to say, "Because God told me…" This is why I am willing to dedicate my life to the glory of God and make Him proud to call me His own. He has done too much for me to make Him my little secret.

Of course I'm nervous that people won't receive what I have to say. Of course I'm nervous that others will judge me harshly. Of course I'm nervous that people will form the wrong conclusions about me. And I'm nervous about potential changes in the way I may have to live. However, I constantly remind myself that I do not live to serve men; I live to serve my Father in Heaven. One day I will have to answer to Him. He will show me my life, the good and the bad. He will determine my fate right then and there. With that being said, I will do everything in my power to make sure that I will hear, "Well done, my good and faithful servant."

I didn't always know my purpose in life. I wanted to know so desperately. I prayed and prayed, asking God to reveal it to me as clear as day. I was just so uncomfortable and unsettled, and I couldn't explain why. I didn't feel happy. I felt like I was just sitting idle while something greater was waiting. Despite my pleading with God, He didn't give me any hints.

I don't know what sparked it, but I had a revelation that seemed so obvious. I knew I was a good at writer, and I knew my writing could help people because it already had. I knew I already had weapons in my artillery, just waiting to be fired. In my mind, I thought, *"I know that I'm good at writing, but is that my gift? Is that how God wants to use me?"* It was like I was playing tug-of-war with God, and God finally just let go of the rope and said, "Here, just take it." He gave up trying to battle with me. He let me figure it out myself. However, once I discovered that writing is how I am supposed to fulfill one of His purposes for my life, He flooded me with affirmations. Even though I pleaded for His revelation, He knew that what I needed was His confirmations once I finally chose to listen. That is what led to the creation of this book.

I want to publicly dedicate this book to my God. You are my rock, You are my peace, You are my joy, and You are my protector and provider. You are my hope and strength, and I will love You and honor You for the rest of my life.

I challenge all who heed these words— believers and non-believers, faithful and unfaithful, strong and weak, young and old —to walk in purpose. What do you contribute to society? What do you put out into the world? If you were to pass away today, would you be remembered and cherished by generations to come? We all have a purpose over our lives, predestined by God. Whether you choose to accept His calling or not is completely up to you. My God is a God of choice; He wants you to choose Him. I can testify that choosing God as the Lord and love of my life has provided me with the strength I need to make it through any storm.

I have fallen victim to lying, hypocrisy, jealousy, drugs, depression, insecurities, betrayal, hurt, idolization, and uncertainty, along with other things. I am no different than anyone else! Our job as believers is to recognize our mistakes, ask for forgiveness and learn our lesson, not repeat the same mistakes, and try to be a mentor and light for others. God created us for the sole purpose of bringing Him glory. In everything that we do, we are required to glorify God.

I have never liked choosing sides. In heated debates that don't concern me, or even in the ones that do, I have always said that I am on the side of truth. I have no loyalty to a particular person in circumstances like that. I'm in favor of everything right. Peep the title. God is the Epitome of everything right. His Word is the definition of truth. Whatever He says, goes. Whatever He proclaims is tried and true. This book is my soul poured onto paper. It is a window into my direct communion with God and the struggles and desires of my flesh. It is extreme vulnerability like I never imagined possible for myself. However, God achieves the impossible, even in the lesser of us.

I am happy to be able to give you this gift. My prayer is that this book reaches whomever it needs to reach, touches whomever needs to be touched, lifts up whomever is feeling low, gives hope to whomever is feeling hopeless, and relates to whomever is feeling guilty about the flaws that make us all human. I will forever be on the side of truth. I will forever be on the winning team. I will forever be *In Favor of Everything Right.* Enjoy.

Nyah J Peyton

Acknowledgments

To my family and friends who
have supported me and
helped me learn myself.

To my God who has given me
many gifts to glorify Him

Comes Down To Judgement

Year 2014

Don't let the sickness and wickedness of this world cloud your way of thinking,
Don't let the cruel and unholy images blur your vision of victory.
Don't let the wrong doings control your temple,
For there comes a day for God to say,
Who comes home and who has to stay.
Don't let this world be a distraction to the plan God has in store.
Let's not pay attention anymore.
You have the power and the will to say "no"
To whatever it is the devil has to throw.
It's coming soon, it's as plain as day.
With all the selfish unholy sin that's taken away.
So be aware and get it right,
As I sit and hold my pillow tight and think about how I can better my life.
I want to go to heaven, but with every life lesson,
I find myself failing.
Pastor says if I believe in my heart and confess with my tongue,
He'll welcome me with open arms.
I hear the church family speak testimonies on how God kept them from harm.
When I witness sin, I try to stay calm, but there's no denying the sweating of my palms.
So be aware, for there comes a day, when God will say,

Who comes home and who has to stay.

There comes a point in every believer's life when you realize that not everyone is going to heaven. You begin to reflect on all of your mistakes and shortcomings, and there in the pit of your gut, you know that if you continue in the direction that you're headed, you might not make the cut.

In the early stages of my life, I self-reflected more than the average eighth grader. Most of my middle school years, I felt out of place. What was weird though, is that I had a lot of confidence in myself. I had confidence in my appearance, my athletic abilities, my likability, my intelligence, and my faith. I felt out of place in the midst of all of this because I didn't feel heard. I didn't feel like my voice mattered. I thought I was a nuisance and that my opinion was irrelevant. This derived from years of playing a certain role at my school. I was supposed to be the funny black girl. When I had real opinions and something important to say, I was ignored. That experience led to me journaling.

I journaled EVERYTHING. Literally. One entry had one sentence about me having to pee in the middle of class. Not all of the entries were this useless and unimportant though. Matter of fact, this poem was an eighth grade journal entry. It signified the beginning of my personal journey with God. I didn't even know it at the time, and I never would have guessed how turbulent this journey would become.

The ideas in this poem line up with the idea of purpose through Jesus Christ. I knew early on that there would "come a day for God to say who comes home and who has to stay." I knew I didn't want to stay here.

This, Too.

Year 2016

God said this too shall come to pass.
My mind, my soul, my heart, want to sing "Free at Last",
But my confidence and my conscience can't seem to grasp.
The emotional toil is becoming a burden;
it's like trying to mix water with oil.
Can't you see that I'm hurting?
It's written on my face, it's present in my stance.
My heart quickens in pace, I clench my hands.
Verbally abused, my predators amused.
The look on my face makes them feel like they've won first place.
No, it's not always obvious to see,
But if you look closer, into my eyes,
My soul is screaming,
PLEASE STOP HURTING ME.
Disappointment in the ones who I thought were different,
Appreciation for the ones who are.
My life looks like the perfect picture,
But I feel like the smallest of all the stars.
Overlooked, undercooked.
Easily shook, a dusty book.
I'm feeling the pain without the gain.
The lesson without the question.

The kite without the string.

The car that has run out of gasoline.

But thank you, Lord, for keeping me alive.

Remove all pain and strife and help me live my life knowing that I'm putting up a good fight.

Just give me a little more strength, that's all I need to help me

Get through this mental struggle.

Because God said

This, too,

Shall come to pass.

Fast forward to my tenth grade year. A lot had happened since the first communion I had with God. I played AAU basketball, I transferred schools, I made new friends, and lastly I met depression. It stared me right in my face every day. Most of my writing during this period was therapeutic, spilling my innermost thoughts out on paper. I didn't realize at the time that I wrote this poem that I was depressed. I just knew I didn't feel good or like myself.

When I transferred to Little Rock Central High School, I knew almost nobody. I knew a handful of people in the general population, and the rest were athletes. I played basketball and soccer, and had played them for the majority of my life. I had played competitive soccer since I was 10 years old, but I had just finished up my first summer of AAU basketball the summer going into tenth grade. Most of the teammates on the Central basketball team were also my AAU teammates. So, going into the program, I was accustomed to the players I was familiar with. What I wasn't accustomed to was the lack of structure the program had. We were a great basketball team, and we won often, but there was a great deal of tension between the players, and verbal abuse was not uncommon.

I am the type of person who thrives on positivity and encouragement. Our team dynamic significantly lacked both of these attributes. Instead, there was a lot of harsh criticism and hurtful teasing, not only among the players, but from the coaches as well. There was no encouragement, at least not spoken to me. It felt as if nothing I did was right. Nothing was good enough for anyone. I would come home every day from practice upset. Every single day. Not only did I feel useless and incompetent on the court, I felt the same way in the classroom. I was having a hard time in school for the first time in my life. I felt so empty and unimportant.

When I wrote this poem, I wrote it as a plea to my teammates to simply stop hurting me. I could feel my spirit being crushed every day. I knew that if something didn't change soon, I would fall into a pit that only God could remove me from. From this point on, my life started to change. I came out of character, and I wasn't nice anymore. I grew too thick of a skin, so thick that I didn't feel anymore. I no longer showed empathy, nor did I care about how I made other people feel.

One day, we had a game, prior to which the opposing team got on social media and said they would beat us by 30 points. We took that completely to heart and that night we beat them by 15 points. Instead of being satisfied by our win, we as a team took to social media and threw a bunch of shade at the other team. They weren't completely innocent though because they threw it right back. Things got a little heated.

Both teams started going back and forth, getting very disrespectful toward each other. I got involved and talked a bunch of head to players on the other team in defense of myself and my teammates. I said some hurtful things, thinking it was funny. I was being fueled through our team group-chat, and for some reason I felt like it was my lady-tiger duty to talk smack.

Well, a couple of days later, my parents found out. One of the players on the other team was the biological niece of my step-uncle all the way in Louisiana. The player showed her mother, her mother recognized the last name Peyton, asked my step-uncle if I was related to my aunt. Then my step-uncle showed my aunt, who showed my father, who showed my mother. Yes, it was a long chain of snitching. I got in a lot of trouble to say the least.

My parents explained to me the importance of keeping your nose clean and not posting things like that on social media. They told me that it was bigger than some beef over a basketball game, I was potentially jeopardizing my future and the opportunities that I could have. I understood 100%. I apologized to the players I had offended, and I deleted all of my tweets. My phone was still taken away. What's worse, my parents replaced it with a flip phone. I had that flip phone for five months. Even in the midst of feeling left out, I was grateful for the punishment, and I knew I deserved it.

However, this was the tip of the iceberg for my battle with depression. I absolutely hate disappointing people. At this point in time, I felt like a major disappointment to my family.

A Lil Extra tidbit:

I just recently discovered the reason behind one of my triggers. During this period of time, when something would happen, my dad would barely look at me and he would shake his head in the utmost disappointed way. This always made me cry and feel even worse.

A short time ago, I was driving through the Hobby Lobby parking lot, and I was about to enter into one of the main thoroughfares. I checked both ways and didn't see anybody coming. As I was pulling out, I checked one more time. I looked left first and then right, and had to slam on my breaks. A man driving an SUV came zooming around the corner and he had to swerve a little bit to keep from getting hit. I started apologizing as if he could hear me. I watched him pass by, subconsciously looking for him to show any signs of irritation or disappointment. There it was. The head shake that I was looking for. I immediately erupted with anger, offended that he shook his head at me. My friend, Faith, was in the car with me, and she quickly asked me why I was tripping. I told her that I didn't like him shaking his head at me. She kept trying to tell me that he shook his head at me, because I almost hit him and he had the right away. All I kept saying was, *"you're right, you're right."*

I was thinking about this moment for the rest of the day. I was embarrassed that I lost my temper, and was upset that I didn't know why I lost it so easily in that moment. As I was taking a shower, it hit me (I have a lot of epiphanies in the shower). I realized that someone shaking their head at me was a trigger that I didn't even know I had. I realized that it stemmed from my father shaking his head at me when I was going through that rough transition all the way back in 10th grade. When I got out of the shower, I texted Faith and explained to her what I had just realized, and apologized to her for reacting the way I did and for possibly making her feel uncomfortable.

There are a lot of things that we experience in the past that we let dictate how we live in and react to situations in the present. I was subconsciously letting my past have power over my temper and my emotions. As much as we want to use the past as an excuse to justify why we do what we do and think the way that we think, we need to make a conscious effort to grow, adjust, and to be the best versions of ourselves possible.

She's Different, So Treat Her Different / I Lost a Special Prize

Year 2018

Who is She?
Complete strangers come to approach Her.
They fluff Her hair and admire her eyes.
Complete strangers say that She is different.
They make Her smile with compliments and serenade Her with rhymes.
Complete strangers want to be with Her,
But they've never spent the time of day.
Butterfly wings in the wind,
Catching the drift of the breeze, but to you I say,
Who are you?
That you are above these strangers?
That you are blind to the marvelousness of Her?
Do you call yourself cool or chilled as a frosted stone?
She tells you the frost will melt soon,
And you will look back irate with your mistake,
That you let the best thing go.
And she didn't just walk, but ran away.

Who is She?

She doesn't seem to be like the others,
The ones who admire my talent to the point of fandom.
She doesn't seem to want to fancy my needs,
Like the ones who cater to my every desire.
She listens and doesn't interrupt when I'm speaking,
She likes to try new things.
She has a surprise for every day and says "no peeking."
She is beautiful naturally and carries herself like a queen, so
Who am I?
To not acknowledge Her efforts to be kind to me,
Even when I was cold toward Her.
Would I forgive me if I was in Her shoes?
Probably not.
To not give Her the attention and affection that She deserves,
She merits more than what I can provide.
And She already knows Her worth,
Her confidence never hides.
So who am I to go back and forth trying to decide?
Now I lost the best thing and I know I made a mistake.

She didn't just walk, but She ran away.

I have always been very respectful of myself. When it comes to my body and time especially, I limit the amount of people I allow into my space and schedule. To this day, I have never had a legitimate boyfriend. Part of that is because of my pickiness, but the major factor is the standards I set. I don't ask for a whole lot, but at the age of 19, it would take an outstanding young man to fulfill my version of a partner: intelligent, considerate, fun, kind, respectful, trustworthy, loyal, and loves Jesus. In my mind, that's the bare minimum. These are the characteristics I am not willing to compromise. I already developed these standards and expectations at the tender age of 14 years old. Now y'all tell me what kind of 14-year-old has all of that? On top of the standards, I wasn't easily flattered. I was picky and didn't really have a lot of interest in people. I can count on one hand how many boys I've had a strong enough interest in, to the point of liking them. Literally, five fingers.

So just imagine the anxiety of admitting that you like a person, to that person's FACE. I'm talking about a full-fledged panic attack. I'm talking about heart beating out of my chest, shortness of breath, sweating, you name it. In my poem *Small Cup*, I describe a little about how I felt when

I actually did suck it up and admit feelings for someone that I had interest in.

This poem is before the actual event. This was the stage of "he's gonna lose this good thing if he doesn't just make a move already" because I definitely don't like making the first move. I'm a very "nah, you got it" type of person. I don't allow myself to be vulnerable like that, I don't like giving people a window or opportunity to hurt me.

I'm working on my willingness to be vulnerable, and I'm doing a lot better. Producer and New York Times Best-selling author, DeVon Franklin, accepted me on his Instagram Live one night, and he said something that countered my hesitance: "Vulnerability leads to victory." I let this resonate with me. Every time I would have an urge to be vulnerable and God would be telling me to testify, I tried to suppress it with a hard-shelled resistance. I now let myself be open and vulnerable, which sometimes makes me uncomfortable, but for the most part, it's been working for me. Sometimes I wish I had these revelations sooner. However, without the rainy days, I wouldn't have gained the early wisdom I have now, nor would I have created the art that has derived from those circumstances.

This piece is two separate poems written from two different perspectives. The first perspective, *She's Different, So Treat Her Differen*t, is written from my viewpoint, aka the girl's view. The second perspective, *I Lost a Special Prize*, is written from the presumed viewpoint of the boy. Even though it was supposed to reflect the standing of the male, it was still written from my perspective, and you can tell that from the verbiage. He wouldn't say that if there was a gun to his head. He's that type of stubborn. These poems were written in my creative writing class, but I didn't treat them like an assignment. In fact, I nearly missed the objective. However, I was happy with the results, and it made the cut to go in this book.

"I"

Year 2019

When a lot is going on around me,
It's easy to become distracted.
It's easy to say what I want and to do as I please, without realizing what all is impacted.
It's easy to put others' needs before my own,
It's easy to ignore the good things in front of me, only to realize when they're gone.
I don't realize the changes that take place in my life until I feel trapped in my own mind.
I don't realize the changes in myself until I hit a wall and am forced to look behind.
I don't pray anymore because I can't find the time, and
I seclude myself from everyone else, all while being lonely and wishing to socialize.
On some days I feel like conquering the world,
But on most I'm too tired to even go to sleep,
Like the idea of dreaming is too great of a leap.
Instead I get to thinking…
Thinking of all of the pain and stress and mess that I've been through.
Thinking of all the times where it should've ended differently, but God spared me.
Thinking of all the times that I literally felt my heart break,
Thinking about each breath that I take,
Keeping count of them in a sorry attempt to meditate.
When a lot is going on around me, it's easy to forget who I am.
I begin to dig deep, only to realize I'm digging in the wrong direction.
I begin to search for answers in all of the places I can think to look,
but all I uncover is more questions.

I start to not care about much.
My emotions are a closed book.
I heavily guard my heart, so it won't get took.
I play songs that I feel are written about me just to feel a connection.
Wishing for, but turning away, intimate attention.
I get bored of people I don't have love for —
You either get all or none of my affection.
I always say "heaven me, please," and I mean it.
Lord when I fulfill my purpose, get me out of here with apprehension.
I'm living life with a sense of urgency,
Like every day is an emergency.
My sirens blare, they're loud and clear, like I'm going into surgery.
Surgery on my mind, a checkup for my soul,
My heart is sick and my symptoms don't show.
No doctor can tell me what's wrong, so I self -diagnose.
When a lot is going on around me, it's easy to become distracted.
It's easy to
Say what I want and do as I please,
Think about other people's needs,
Ignore the good things in front of me,
Not realize the changes,
Stop praying,
Feel lonely while socializing,
Stop sleeping, so no dreaming, and to
Think of my heart breaking.
When a lot is going on around me it's easy to forget who I am.

I begin to

Dig in the wrong direction,

Search for answers and instead find questions,

Stop caring,

Get bored,

Long for a connection,

Crave certain attention,

Wish I was in heaven,

Realizing an emergency,

Acting in urgency,

Feel symptoms unseen, and to

Diagnose that my spirit is dying.

The best advice I can give to me is to

Make sure I stay away from a lot of things.

In my writing, I have a tendency to talk in second person. I use phrases like "you" instead of "I," even though I'm talking about myself. It was almost like a way of deflecting my emotions and projecting them onto the general population. I wrote this poem sitting in my car in the back of a Whole Foods parking lot. I was alone and didn't want to be. For a while, I sat there in silence, waiting on my friend to text me when she got home. Sadness comes out of silence. Epiphanies also come out of silence.

God placed the first line of my poem in my mind, and it just flowed from there. I was transparent in the way that I expressed myself. I cried as every insecurity I felt at the time spilled out into literary artwork. When I was about halfway through the poem, I realized that I was using the word "you" to describe myself. I thought about the fact that this poem wasn't about "you," it was about Nyah. I went back through the poem and changed every single "you" to an "I" and also made it the title. I decided to take ownership of my emotions.

This was my cry for help. I was admitting defeat and recognizing that I needed healing.

Don't Let Me Go

Year 2020

Depression is something that is so discrete.
It comes when I'm least expecting.
It creeps and sinks into every smile.
I give my feelings an inch, and they take a mile.
Is what I'm feeling relevant, will it help me grow?
Battling with whether expression is even worthwhile.
So in the meantime I fight alone.
Irritation and temper in my tone,
People can tell I'm dealing with something, but don't know what's wrong.
I know I'm feeling something, but the only word I can think to describe it is numb.
Care free, I don't care about much in the world because the world doesn't seem to care much about me.
And I could be wrong.
I know I have the love from my friends and family.
I know God will never leave nor forsake me.
This is why I feel guilty when I say I feel something is missing.
There is no finger to point it out.
No beacon of light or a yellow brick road.
No backpack or partner to help carry the load.
But I continue to trek up the mountain with the faith of finishing,
Confidence in Whom I believe in, and
Comfort in knowing that this is not my final destination,
Simply a mission along the way.
And when I get to heaven someday,

I’m going to thank God that He didn’t let me go.

"Depression is something that is so discrete." I have gone through depression a couple of times. I called it situational depression. I don't even know if that's a real thing, but it described my depression so well. Situational depression is when you find yourself in a depressive state based on a sequence of unfortunate or difficult situations. I know the easiest advice is to just focus on the positive, but it's not that simple when you don't feel connected to God. God says in Galatians 5:12, that without His spirit, we cannot have love, joy, peace, or faithfulness.

I was in a spiritual drought and all of my spiritual fruit was spoiled rotten. I thought I was full of life, full of joy, full of faithfulness and peace. I wasn't aware of my own emptiness. I knew I never wanted to be alone because I felt sad and incomplete, so I was always trying to surround myself with people. "It creeps and sinks into every smile." None of my smiles felt genuine. I never smiled on my own. I only smiled when other people made me smile.

I didn't tell anyone what I was feeling because I didn't know I was feeling it. "Battling with whether expression is even worthwhile. So in the meantime I fight alone." All I knew was that I had a short temper and got easily irritated. I was frustrated that when someone asked me what was wrong, I didn't know how to answer them. "There is no finger to point it out."

I knew God didn't abandon me and that He was watching, even though at the time it didn't feel like it. I was in the middle of a test, a test that would ultimately strengthen my relationship with God. My only prayer was that God wouldn't let me go.

Paranoia

Year 2018

It eats you up from the inside out. Do you know what constant fear is like?
What ‘ bad feeling ’ really means? Scared to go outside or walk down the street,
So you drive yourself, instead of walking, crazy.
But you go, and you see, and you experience what it’s like, that bad feeling.
Fast forward and you think about what could’ve been wrong or different.
You think too hard.
But what if I was alone with just him and, what if I felt the rod of heat come upon me?
What if I wanted to be cold?
That’s not the warmth I pictured when I thought about heat.
The gut-wrenching paranoia of having the guts pushed out of me.
So I would rather drive, than walk myself, crazy because I’m scared of who might be
Walking behind, or in front, or to the sides of me.
I must always be ready because I have precious cargo to protect.
Baggage upon baggage of fine artillery and the finest jewels.
A cluster of unpicked flowers, pure as a baby fresh from their mother's womb.
For every reason they should want to steal my baggage from me,
The men walking behind, or in front, or to both sides of me.
So, I drive myself, instead of walking, crazy.
I know at any moment my baggage could be stolen from me,
My jewels, my flowers, my precious artillery.
And walking makes me more vulnerable to the man carrying the heat.
Let me stay cold please.
I don’t want to be warm right now,

I don’t want to know how it feels or what it’s like,
I said no right now.
And you’re trying to take, what I’m trying to protect;
My artillery, and my jewels, and my flowers, and my smoothness.
That’s why I drive, instead of walk, myself crazy,
Because I’m scared of who might be walking behind, or in front, or to both sides of me.
I release my grip from the dusty curtain.
Bare backs show the fruits of his labor, covered in salty sweat and his fluids,
Bruises that turn plum, the poison of hate turns my heart numb.
But it doesn’t make sense because I drove!
I drove myself crazy, I didn’t walk.
I avoided the strangers walking behind, or in front, or to either side of me.
I did everything I was supposed to, I did everything I could, yet …
My jewelry was stolen. My artillery is no longer precious.
My flowers were picked, and plucked, and pruned, and wilted down to the stem.
I’m no longer cold,
I’m filled with sweltering heat.
No longer the paranoia of who is walking behind, or in front, or to either side of me.
Now I walk in small steps, instead of driving myself crazy,
Because I can never be cold again.

And what was stolen from me can never be returned.

One of my greatest fears is being raped. The disrespect, pervertedness, and pure THIEFISM of it all is just sickening. I know "thiefism" is not a word, but it just adds the intensity I feel towards the whole idea. The theft of "precious artillery." Whether we like it or not, there is very little we can actually control in this world, but one thing we can control is what we do with our bodies. What we feed it, what we do to it, how much we value it. For someone to invade that intimate space and mock the only thing you actually have control over, is one of the worst evils someone can do in my opinion.

I have never been raped, and I pray that I never have to experience it. This poem was written from the base of my fears. *What am I afraid of? What am I doing to try to prevent this from happening to me? How would I feel if this happened to me despite all of the so-called precautionary actions I'm taking?* In reality, I would never know for sure unless I experienced it myself. I hope to never know how it would really feel.

Vulnerable Tranquility

Year 2017

My vulnerability is tranquil, stuck in these feelings that are painful, it's hurting…
It hurts so much, as my heart turns cool to the touch.
I put on my mask and say I'm alright, but it's really nothing as such,
As the knife in my back pierces me through to my guts.
Struggling to find the inner strength to push and pull myself up,
Raising my spiritual glass toward the heavens,
Lord fill my cup,
I can't go through this alone.
Confidence beams through the being of my beauty and it seems as if nothing could phase me,
But you'd think I'm playing and you would call me crazy
If I told you I struggle with my own self-identity.
All these people in my face who want to occupy my space,
But not once have they asked me how I'm doing or if I'm okay.
Females who change up like make-up,
Boys who only speak up when the daylight's up,
People who come knocking when the door is shut,
And when you try to open up, you end up getting cut,
And it's just all too much…

To handle on my own.
At least I have my God so I know I'm not alone.

But it still hurts when you don’t pick up the phone,

Not knowing and/or not caring if something’s wrong.

I want to forgive, I even want to forget,

But the past can’t help but stick.

My memory is clogged with resentful bricks that beat me until the love doesn’t exist.

Vulnerable tranquility,

That's what’s inside of me, don’t know where to move,

Don't know how to speak.

I’m losing myself so that they will love me, you see,

My vulnerability is tranquil, stuck…

In these feelings that are paralyzingly painful.

This journal entry was written right before the poem. This is the straw that broke the camel's back and catapulted me into depression. Some of the names have been changed for the privacy of the individuals:

<u>July 25, 2017</u>

So last year I told ya'll about Breana and Layla and I said they were my best friends. Well, at the time, I honestly thought they were. I felt I could trust them, and I wanted to be around them all the time. I thought that they had the same feelings about me, but I know now that I was wrong. We were all really good friends starting from last AAU season until about March or April of 2017. The last thing we did together was spend a day at Petit Jean Mountain. Shoot, even there I felt left out, and I was the one who invited them. But that night, Breana was kind of emotional, I guess from something Layla said to her, and she started to get attitude-y. I didn't say anything to provoke it, but [Breana] told me to shut up, and she meant it. Anybody who knows me, knows that shut up is NOT in my registry of things that are "okay" to tell me to do. Y'all, I was so mad that I started washing dishes at midnight. I even went to clean my room, even though it was already clean. We all went to sleep mad.

The next morning everybody was fine apparently, except for Breana and Layla. Breana was still mad at Layla for what she said, I guess. After I dropped Layla off at her mom's job, Breana's whole demeanor changed. I later found out that they made up and were buddy-buddy again.

But yeah… that was the last thing we did TOGETHER outside of basketball practice.

Ever since then, I have been … left behind. I wanted to say ignored, but it's not quite that. I get acknowledgement, but only because Layla and I have a streak [on Snapchat], and Breana watches my story.

In July, I decided not to play AAU this year. Something that was supposed to be character-building was character-destroying. At Central, my confidence was snapped in two by Coach Michael. Nothing I did was right in his eyes. I'm the type of kid who thrives off of confirmation. I need acknowledgement of my efforts. I used to always work hard, but after Central, I acquired the mentality that it was pointless for me to give my best, when my best was never enough, so I never tried my hardest or gave my all. When AAU started back up, it was like two weeks after the state final. Coach Ed had tryouts at Pulaski Academy, and I was beyond nervous. All us Central girls were so out of shape because we never ran with Coach Michael and didn't do anything on our own. At the tryout, me, Jo and Erynn were STRUGGLING. Jo and I almost passed out! But I continued to work hard, for Coach Ed. I gave my best … like I had always done for him, since last summer. But once again ladies and gentlemen, my best wasn't enough.

He told me that I wasn't going to sit on the bench at Central and then come run his team. He separated me from everybody my own age, even the other sophomores, and made me play with the 7th - 9th graders. I was so embarrassed … in front of my "friends," in front of the parents, in front of the new people trying out all the hope I had of redemption and confidence-building, and pleasing him and showing everybody that I HAD been working and I HAD gotten better, it all went away, right then. And from that day on, I went back to the Central mentality. I didn't work hard in practice. My body was beginning to fail me due to stress, so I was constantly injured or getting sick in practice and catching muscle cramps.

I fell into a minor depressive state because I felt worthless. During this time, Breana and Layla stopped talking to me. I was trying to get my grades right. I was in trouble and had my phone taken for an extended period of time. I was struggling with self-identity and confidence in my intellectual and physical abilities. There was just TOO much going on at one time. I cried a lot. And I still cry sometimes.

I can't help but try to think of things I could have done differently. Something that could have possibly changed this negative chain of reactions. How could I have done better in basketball so that Coach Michael would like me? How could I have been a better friend so that Layla and Breana would still want to be around me? What could I have possibly done differently at Coach Ed's tryout that would have kept him from belittling me in front of everyone in the gym? All of those questions were ALWAYS weighing heavy on my heart and on my mind.

The day I stopped playing AAU … a day I will never forget, to be honest. Prior to that day, I had been out for two weeks due to an ankle sprain. The first two days of the sprain, I was on crutches and could not apply any pressure. My ankle was swollen for the first week, nearly the size of a baseball. I was limping for that week and half of the next. The first day I was able to run or even jog on that ankle was that day at practice. Of course nobody knew that because nobody bothered to ask me where I had been for the past two weeks, let alone talk to me AT ALL during that time. So, obviously, not being able to condition for the previous two weeks, I was out of shape going into Coach Ed's basketball practice, famously known for being extra tough. I was just happy to be back on the floor and able to play with and see my teammates again. I even told Layla, who was lacing up right next to me, that I was so happy to be back, I didn't even care if we ran. It was true. I knew running was a big part of the game. I didn't like it, but I knew it was necessary.

When practice started, I was doing fine at first. I was winded, but not too tired yet; I was feeling good. Then, apparently Coach Ed didn't like what he was seeing, so he took us outside to the parking lot, something he just recently started doing. We didn't go outside one time last season. But that day, it was so humid out. We ran sprint after sprint. My ankle was throbbing. I couldn't breathe. Still, I ran. I never once stopped running. The feeling of unconsciousness weighed me down, but still I ran. My legs were giving out and only had enough strength to get me from point A to point B, but still I ran. My heart throbbed through my chest due to a lack of oxygen, but still I ran. My ankle, I could feel, was beginning to swell again, so my shoe was getting tight and began to cut off the blood flow in my foot, but still I ran. My arms were heavy and my muscles were beyond fatigued, but still I ran. I had no intention of stopping anytime soon.

My teammates were begging me to quit so they could stop. Coach Ed told me to beat the next group I was running with or it would be double. I beat them and then collapsed onto the concrete, face down, unable to move any muscles. I had just given my all, my best, once again. Not for my rude, inconsiderate, and barking teammates, but for the man I set out to please. I couldn't even breathe properly. All I heard was chastisement and hateful and resentful shouts and orders —from Coach and teammates alike.

"Get up," from Coach Ed. But I couldn't feel my feet. I had no control over my muscles or my body. It was like I had forgotten how to move.

"Nyah, get up!" from Layla, a piercing holler that hurt me to know that I was the cause of my friends" suffering.

"GET UP! GO HOME! You are being SELFISH if you don't go home!" from Mariah, the one everybody likes, including myself.

I had never been on the other side of this mistreatment. Her scream was the worst. It succeeded all of the others and was loud and high-pitched and filled with anger and irritation. I laid there still. I cried. A silent cry so nobody could hear me. A quick sob so nobody would see. A resentful cry which made me feel some type of way. A hurting cry to relieve my heart just a little of the pain it felt.

EVERYTHING in this entry led to that moment, that moment of destruction and defeat. Only recently have I been feeling those feelings. I said something I regret and didn't mean. As adrenaline kicked in and I was able to force myself onto my feet, I said, "I hate them." I said it over and over until I thought I meant it. I knew I didn't, but I wanted to. When I was able to stand, I immediately began to hobble and stumble to the building, looking at no one. I don't remember anybody saying anything, but when I finally looked up, I saw them do their last sprint, then head toward the building. I didn't want to speak to anybody, and I didn't want anybody to speak to me. Layla, Makayla, and Mariah beat me to the gym. I walked in and didn't say a word. My face was cold and resentful, and I could feel it. I grabbed my bag, snatched my keys, and didn't even bother to take off my shoes. I was asked on the way out by somebody's mom if I was okay. I told the most blatant lie I have ever told: "yes ma'am."

When I got inside my car, I broke into sobs. I cried heavy, heavy tears that stained my face and speckled my surroundings. My voice hurt from the deep moans and thrusted screams. My heart hurt, my pride hurt, my mental state was weak, my emotional state was unbalanced, my body was throbbing with a mix of anger and fatigue. When I finally got myself under control, I left —and dreaded having to go back, because I knew the same chastisement would be present. Again, that day, my best wasn't enough. STORY OF MY LIFE.

When I got home I talked with my parents and told them what happened. My dad worried for my mental health, and they both wondered if it was worth putting me through this. That afternoon, after practice, I decided it wasn't. I was tired of being mistreated and bullied. I was tired of being hurt mentally, physically, and emotionally, I was tired of crying over the SAME THING, I was tired of giving my best and it coming back to stab me. [It seemed] nobody wanted me around anyway. I instantly fell into peace when I decided I was done.

I smiled to myself the rest of the day. All while I ate lunch, all while I washed my uniform, all while I told my parents goodbye, all while I drove to practice that evening, all while I laced my shoes, all while I shot on the other end of the court by myself, all while we warmed up, all while I listened to Layla and Breana and knew in my heart that the friendship wouldn't be the same anytime soon, all while Jaylen was begging me to stay, all while I shot the last free throw to keep us from running. But … when it was time to leave, and I brought out the freshly washed uniform, my smile went away and tears welled up. Jaylen, my best friend, saw my distress and grabbed me.

We sat and talked in the back of the hallway on the floor. She tried her best to make me feel better and to support my decision, but she was still begging me to reconsider. When it was finally time to go, our conversation was cut short by Coach Ed calling for her. We snuck back into the gym through the back door and she lied and said her shoes were misplaced and she had to find them. I stayed behind, sitting by myself, looking around at the gym and thinking about good things. I saw [Coach] Dae Dae come around the corner and he told Coach Ed I was still in there.

Coach Ed came to me. I tried to hand him my uniforms, but I could barely speak through my tears and lumped throat. I finally got it out that I couldn't do this anymore. This phrase opened up a half-hour conversation. Coach Ed did most of the talking. I had never seen this side of him before, the side that cared. He told me to sleep on it and come back next practice, or however long I needed, to tell him what the deal was. I slept on it alright. I almost reconsidered simply because I saw that he actually DID care. Somebody cared! But I still decided I needed a mental, emotional, and physical break. It had been a long year …

(END OF JOURNAL ENTRY)

I am the type of person to blame myself for things that happen to me. I always take full ownership, even when it's not my fault. I used to feel like there was always SOMETHING that I could have done differently in order to change the trajectory of the outcome of a situation. In time, I came to accept that yes, while my actions do cause reactions, sometimes things cannot be avoided, especially if it is in God's will.

I lost some friends during this period in my life. I thought I had done something that made them not like me anymore. I was beating myself up over it. Eventually, I understood that it wasn't me. There was nothing I could have done differently to change anything that went on during that time.

I was hurt, and I had been done wrong. It took a while for me to be able to admit that because I love Breana and Layla. In the following months, I discovered more and more about how they felt about me and yes, it did break my heart. However, I forgave them. I will always be there when they need me, I will always be there to encourage them, I am always in their corners. Even though I forgive them, I will never forget. Never forgetting doesn't mean holding a grudge or holding something over their heads. For me, it means that I will not allow myself to forget because I don't want to fall victim to the same situation, and be naively sucked back into something familiar. I forgave them a long time ago; it's all love this way. In the long run, I grew from this experience and learned what type of friend I DIDN'T want to be. I would consider this a blessing in disguise. Out of this storm, I derived my mantra: *Be kind to everyone.* Seems cliché, but treat people the way you want to be treated. I knew then, and I know now, that I never want anyone to feel the way I felt in 2017. In all of my friendships, I make sure that I pay attention to the other person. I make them feel special, let them know they are valuable to me, and that I love them, I enjoy their company, and that they will always have a friend in me.

B.W.B.G. (Beautiful, Wonderful Black Girl)

Year 2020

Beautiful black girl,
Keep your faith.
Keep your confidence and self-worth;
That's what it's gonna take to run this race.

Wonderful black girl,
Masked with an ebony face.
God hears your prayers
And His timing has a perfect pace.

Worrying black girl,
Stop your wishing and sighing.
Be the change you want to see;
There is no time for crying in self-pity.

Beautiful black girl,
Trouble doesn't last always.
Sometimes you need the dark clouds
So you can appreciate the better days.

Wonderful black girls,
Hold your heads up high!
Let your light so shine,
Let it burst through your eyes.

For there is no other as beautiful as you are.

Dedicated To The B.W.B.G.'s in My Life:

Yolanda Peyton
Arlene Gillam
Jewel Peyton
Kendal Peyton
Chanda Lewis
Cynthia Moore
Tyra Gillam
Lorece Bright-Berry
Beata Lovelace
Kimberly Gillam
Stacey McAdoo
Jalinska Gillam
Wanda Keith
Kiley Dulaney
Faith Pinell
Jada Blunt
Lajarlyn Wesley
Myia McBride
Kaleena Jones
Kameelah Harris
Holly Jointer
Michelle Dulaney
Tabitha Hall

Brania Levi
Iris Gillam
Kamya Willis
Skylar West
Bailie Blackman
Connie McGowan
Brooklyn Robinson
Beyoncé Knowles-Carter
Issa Rae
Tyra Gillam
Kai Gillam
Trolicia Johnson
Jasmine Morrow
Kayla Maxwell
Kinylah Newsome
Catherine Wilson
Bre'Amber Scott
Gifte Pavatt
Adaja Cooper
Marshayla Rhodes
Laniyah Trice
Rhyan Curtis
Yvonne Orji

Shelby Ellison
Bailey Ellison
Jordan Greenwood
Makiyah Stephens
Paige Mitchell
Tonie Gaddie
Sha Spencer
Annette Fisher
Lajuana Lovelace
Reya Mosby
Asia Deloach
Kaya Blount
Tomijah Smith
Ralynn Rand
Char Duppins
Shanna Shavers
Cherith Williamson
Katherine Woziwodzki
Michaela Crenshaw
Erin Jacks
Madra Harden
Jada Simpson
Luvvie Jones

Kyrah Bailey	Meagan Good-Franklin	Mariyah Green
Jamee McAdoo	Lauryn Pendleton	Elyse Smith
Kamaria Russell	Morgan Miller	Alexis Forney
Jaylen McGowan	Kennedy Fields	Elva Cromwell
Reagan Bradley	Billynda McAdoo	Amori Anthony
Jaylen Mallard	Kanara Shirley	Kaliyah Rogers
Chloe Bailey	Caliyah McDonald	Zainab Shah
Carla Montgomery	Alexia Crater	Tamara Carpenter
Travicka Keaton	Shanetta Agnew	Makayla Estes
Joscelyn Tillman	Denise Estes	Khadija Estes
Christyn Williams	Jasmine Blunt	Jennifer Montgomery
Aisha Foster	HONORARY: Andrea Gillam	

Small Cup

Year 2019

How does he have this much power over me?
People say others can't get into your head unless you allow them to be.
But who told him he was allowed?
Nobody.
Nobody but me, at least.
And you can't take what I say with a grain of salt because I change my mind quickly.
Feelings get hurt easy.
Pride gets checked and my face starts thumping.
My eyes get heavy, but I don't feel like crying.
Thinking about what I said and regretting.
Feeling regret that I even let you know like that, which I never do.
Emotions very surface, very much 1 + 1 equals 2,
But for some reason, I found myself opening up to you.
I thought it was a great idea initially, all nervous and feeling tingly.
Anxious to see what you might say in response to me.
Then the answer comes, but it's what's unexpected.
You say something that hurts unexpectedly.
I don't know why I care so much, I don't like how it feels.
Like your chest is crushed.
Squeezed tight up.
Like a balled up fist fitting in a small cup.
Then you get angry.
To hell with anger; you just fed up.

By you I mean me, I get fed up so easily.

But this... this is different.

Now you're already treating me differently.

I regret telling you, I reminisce regretfully.

I see how people become alcoholics; it makes you forget what's going on.

Your mind slips and you act forgetfully, not remembering how it makes you feel.

You block every feeling.

Then you come down from the temporary.

Might as well stay down permanently because that hurt ain't going nowhere.

And recently, I've been thinking a lot.

I've been thinking a lot lately.

Overthinking maybe, whatever you wanna call it.

But you're thought provoking.

I think about the attention I've been getting.

Not from you but everyone else around me.

You will never realize how annoyed I am.

It's the most annoying thing.

I thought it was a great idea initially, all nervous and feeling tingly.

Anxious to see what you might say in response to me.

Then the answer comes, but it's what's unexpected.

You say something that hurts unexpectedly.

I don't know why I care so much, I don't like how it feels.

Like my chest is crushed.

Squeezed tight up.

Like a balled up fist fitting in a small cup.

Allowing myself to be vulnerable has always been hard for me to do. It felt like every time I tried, it would come back to bite me later. After talking to my mother, I let her convince me to be vulnerable with the boy I was interested in at the time. I saw so many red flags, so many character flaws, but I decided to try. I had settled on the notion that he had potential, he had the right intentions and a good heart.

Long story short, I invited him to lunch before I went to work and when we sat down, I immediately got nervous. He kept questioning me and asking if he had done something wrong, like he always did. I kept assuring him he didn't do anything wrong and that I was nervous. Eventually —after eating all of my food and drinking two glasses of water —I sucked it up and released. I was sweating the whole time, my voice was shaking, and I couldn't even look him in the face. When I was finished, I just looked at him, searching his face for any sign that he would say something that I would like to hear. Much to my dismay, it was the opposite: "I don't know why I care so much, I don't like how it feels. Like your chest is being crushed. Squeezed tight up like a balled up fist fitting into a small cup."

I wasn't used to caring about what a boy felt about me. I was almost mad at myself for caring. I will never forget how I felt. It was literally like a ball in my chest. I wrote this poem on the way back from The University of Arkansas Fayetteville homecoming weekend. I was riding in the passenger seat, and I wanted to take a nap. I couldn't go to sleep, though. I just had a tug and pull to write. Then it hit me, "How does he have this much power over me?" From that sentence on, I wrote "Small Cup". I completed the poem in about 15 minutes. When I was done, I was able to sleep like a baby.

The Wall

Year 2020

My mother said I built a wall.
I guess I always knew, but I didn't notice until now.
The fear of vulnerability barricades out the possible love of my life.
The bridge only let down to allow friends over the moat of
Dry texts, cut ties, and fronts of "I don't care's."
She said I built a wall because I've been hurt before.
This is true.
I let a man across that moat and onto my bridge, into my fortress,
My fortress of vulnerability.
He was let in, then spit out.
He was caught trying to steal my heart, my happiness, and my confidence.
A thief, he was.
My wall goes up and the bridge begins to burn as he walks across.
Every five steps forward, he takes six steps backward, to avoid the flames licking at his ankles.
I watch him struggle from my fortress,
Wanting him to just leap instead of walk, so he can make it to the other side.
But he's afraid.
My mother said I should tear my wall down…
To allow him in.
To allow myself to be hurt, to allow myself to be happy, to allow myself to experience,
To allow myself to love.

When it comes to men, I have a low-to-no tolerance for foolishness. I am wise beyond my years when it comes to relationships. I don't know everything about everything, but I do in fact know exactly what I want. I do know what I can and cannot tolerate. I can count on one hand how many men I've actually liked in my lifetime so far. I guess I can call them boys because first of all, I'm super young. I'm only 19 years old at the writing of this book, but my birthday is in November, so by the time it is published and distributed, I'll be 20. Anyway, the fact of the matter is, I was setting unrealistic expectations for a bunch of baby boys. That is one of the reasons why I have yet to have a boyfriend. I used to want one, but right now that's not my focus. I am absorbed in God, then my life, school, and family. Anything other than those are not a priority at the moment.

My mom always told me that I had a wall up when it came to boys. I didn't like to be vulnerable or sensitive with them. I was quick to spot what I didn't like instead of what I did like. I had this childhood friend that I had kind of rekindled a relationship with. Nothing intimate, just cool. We went on casual dates, and we talked often. We worked out together and he would come to some of my basketball games and vice versa. Over time, I found myself becoming interested in the idea of being more than just friends with him, but I was afraid to admit it. I was afraid that if I admitted it and he didn't feel the same way, that I would lose his friendship. (Side note: The poem entitled "Small Cup" is about the outcome of this situation.) I told my mother, and we had this long conversation about not being afraid to be vulnerable. "The fear of vulnerability barricades out the possible love of my life." I wanted to let him in, but I was so hesitant. Eventually I did, but it definitely came back to slap me in my face later. Long story short, God gave me the clarity I needed. We never got together, and we are no longer friends. This poem is about my wall.

Ode to My Heart

Year 2017

Ode to my heart for you are beautiful.
You're pure, yet polluted,
For you have been marveled upon by many,
But you have also been exposed to the weights of the world.
Your happiness overflows at times,
And at other times, it's dry like a California drought.
It sings and doesn't care about opinions.
It dances, but doesn't know all of the steps.
It jumps for joy, but can't touch the rim.
It loves unconditionally.
Ode to my heart for you are complicated.
Sometimes you desire things that are bad for you,
You love the things that don't show you love.
Too many times you have been bruised,
But you bandage the bruises.
Too many times you have been misused,
But you find hope to cling to.
You forgive easily,
You never forget,
But a grudge in the ventricles of your whole doesn't exist.
Ode to my heart for you are red.
Red like the blood that pumps through you,
Flowing like hot lava that provides the heat when you run,

The heat when you love,

The heat when you're angry,

The heat when you're nervous,

The heat when you're embarrassed,

The heat when you're flattered,

Ode to my heart for you are different.

You are good to others like you are good to me.

No prejudice or judgement,

Impossible!

You have faith in untrustworthy beings,

Impossible!

You're blind to the ugliest adjectives,

Impossible!

You achieve the impossible,

For you are different.

Ode to my heart for you are special.

Missing Link, Missing Piece

Year 2020

When You disconnected, You took a piece of me with You.
A piece I've tried to, but cannot replace.
There's too much depth, too much intricacy, in this empty space.
How do I celebrate a day of love when I'm missing one.
I haven't even seen the ones I really love faces.
No mountain or moon can fill this void that's been created.
Tolerable friendships I've learned to create.
Surrounded by people every day, but I still feel lonely.
You don't understand why I don't want to be alone.
When I'm alone, I feel empty.
The part of me that's You, is missing.
The only thing that I can't have,

I need.

The feeling of disconnection from God when He was previously so present, is sickening. It's enough to make you cry out. It leaves you feeling empty and lost. Until you experience this specific feeling, you will never understand why I was willing to lose people, things, and my life to reconnect with Him. I wanted nothing more during this time but to feel Him in my spirit again.

I first realized the disconnect when I would pray and would feel like I was talking to the air. Zero movement in my spirit. They were empty prayers. I had never felt that feeling before. In time, I discovered how and why the disconnection occurred.

I'm embarrassed to admit anything that portrays me as anything contrary to how I want to be perceived. However, God commands that I remove me and replace myself with Thee. So, here goes nothing.

When I started college, I was excited about the freedoms that came from the independence of living on campus. I knew that this independence included going wherever I wanted, whenever I wanted. The first semester was an absolute movie. I went to parties and kickbacks, which is fine, but I was irresponsibly doing so. I would drink at some of these kickbacks. In October of 2019, I smoked my first blunt. Toward the end of the semester, I went to less and less parties and kickbacks, and instead replaced them with smoke sessions. I psyched myself out and compared myself to other people, trying to justify myself: “At least I don’t smoke everyday like so-and-so,” or “at least I have a relationship with God and go to church on Sunday,” or “at least my grades are still good.” I used these excuses as justifications.

One of the largest mistakes I’ve made in my life thus far, was ignoring my own conscience. Every time I smoked, I couldn’t help but think about how disappointed my parents would be if they found out, how disappointed I was in myself for succumbing to temptation, and how disappointed God was in me. However, from the outside looking in, it seemed like I didn’t care.

One day, I had one of many realizations. I figured out that the reason I felt so disconnected from God was because I was destroying, vandalizing, and polluting His temple. God cannot coexist with evil. Either He is within you, or He isn’t. Even though God was present in my life and was keeping me in times when I should've been harmed, I felt my personal relationship with Him disappear the more I smoked. So that day, I decided I was taking a break. God put it on my heart to begin studying the book of Romans, and during this time, He required me to be completely sober. I had a good start, but I didn't keep it up.

After about a week and a half, I could feel God's presence creep back into my conscience and my spirit. My prayers didn't feel empty, and I was happier. It was short-lived, of course, because I got too comfortable. I lasted two weeks. I didn't finish my Bible Study and I started gradually smoking again. I went right back to what I was doing before —like a dummy.

The next time I felt the disconnect, it was even worse than the first time.

I wrote this poem on Valentine's Day, a day that was supposed to be about love, but I felt neglected. I felt like God deserted me. I knew He loved me, but I no longer sensed it. Scariest thing ever. "The part of me that is You, is missing. The only thing that I can't have, I need". I needed God, and I felt like I couldn't reach Him. He was my missing link, my missing piece. Hence, the title.

In February of 2020, I finally listened. God had been telling me for weeks that I needed to stop smoking so that He could work through me. Ironically enough, He told me this when I was as high as a kite. I was sitting in the passenger seat of my friend's car and couldn't hear anything. I literally went deaf. I couldn't feel anything either. I closed my eyes and focused on my breathing. In that moment, I felt Him. His voice was so soothing, yet it was heavy at the same time. He said to me, "You need to stop. You can't do this anymore." I opened my eyes and just stared ahead of me. I can't remember much from that evening, I just remember that was my last time smoking.

Since then, God's presence is no longer missing from my conscience and my life. I vowed to myself before that I would never smoke. I renewed my vow. There is no reward, there is no fulfillment, there is no comfort —the consequences are too great. I need God, I need to hear His voice. I will never let anything come between us again.

Puzzle

Year 2020

I tolerate a lot of stuff.
Situations, people, myself.
But at what point can I absorb into something?
Warp into someone?
At what point does everything start to fit?
Puzzles take time to complete,
Especially ones with thousands of pieces.
Or a few, possibly.
Looking at the bigger picture may not be so clear,
And the cover on the box doesn't make it any easier.
The box is fraud.
The picture? A faced.
It warps into a different image when my face steers away.
The puzzle which is impossible to complete,

can only help you patiently tolerate more things.

"But at what point can I absorb into something? Warp into someone?" Feeling purposeless sucks. Like you're just taking up valuable space with invaluable existence. I looked at life like a puzzle that had no box. You know how the picture on the box shows you exactly what the end result is supposed to look like in order for you to complete the puzzle faster? Yeah, life doesn't have one of those. The box that the puzzle pieces of life came in was like a kaleidoscope picture, constantly warping and changing into something different.

"The puzzle which is impossible to complete, can only help you patiently tolerate more things." Life isn't a puzzle. Puzzles are predictable and absolute, quite the opposite of life. I was trying to navigate and maneuver through life without God. I FAILED. Obviously. I was desperate to know what I was here for. I just wanted to be somebody, feel something, feel like some of the pieces were finally starting to line up and fit together. I tolerated 'fake' for way too long. I just wanted to be something and feel something real. I knew God was real, and I knew the love of and from my family was real, but I didn't know what else was real outside of those things.

Finally, I accepted that I didn’t have to have everything figured out yet. I didn’t have to view life that way. Rather, I have to be patient and do my part to become better; meet God halfway, instead of sitting around waiting on Him to perform a miracle. I neglected the puzzle.

Timing

Year 2020

Beautiful girl, skin of smooth stone and pearl.
Lips of feathers and tears of rose water.
Smile of gold, eyes of crystals.
Hair of silken wool.
Mind of knives, sharp and deadly.
Ears of rationality, nose of wisdom.
Your arms and legs pillars of marble, heart of gelatin.
Your back is a slab of granite, proven to be strong.
Trying to carry the weight of your thoughts of steel, lips are sealed.
Lungs of fire.
Breast of valor.

Only be brave when you have to be.

"Only be brave when you have to be." Praise yourself, acknowledge God's beautiful creation. It's okay to be vulnerable, you don't have to be strong all of the time. You don't always have to be brave. You don't always have to suppress your tears. There is a time for bravery, and there is a time for strength. This poem was inspired by the strong black women in my life who have proven time and time again that they are seemingly invincible. This poetic letter highlights their strength, but also invites them into the warm cushion of vulnerability.

Hypocrite

Year 2020

Hypocrite,
You can't learn a lesson.
You aren't allowed to make mistakes.
You have not been given the permission to be given grace.
Hypocrite,
You can't be wise.
You can't learn from what you've been through,
Because what you've been through and
What you have done define you.
Oh hypocrite,
I thought you were holy.
I thought you were the epitome of Bible beating.
I thought you were good.
I thought you would do better than me,
You aren't a normal human being.
You hypocrite.
Your hands are unclean,
Your nose is dry,
And your eyes don't gleam with light.
You hypocrite.
You don't retaliate,
You won't get angry,

Your feelings are impenetrable,

You never make a mistake.

OH YOU HYPOCRITE!

I thought you were Godly and holy,

Someone who doesn't even need grace.

But now as I see the truth plastered on your face, you are just like the rest of us.

The difference between you and me is that you know better, you just don't do better.

What a hypocrite.

I don't care too much for hypocrites. I don't care too much for people who expect Christians to be perfect, to never make mistakes. I don't care too much for people who don't let others learn their lessons in peace. I don't care too much for those people. I had a conversation with some friends from high school, and they have a way of making you discredit your lessons and trials. They have a way of making you feel hypocritical.

There was this trend going around where there was a circle cut up into several sections, and if you put some money in it, you would come out with eight times what you had invested, as long as you could recruit other people to join it and keep it alive. That is definitely the condensed version — I know y'all are probably confused —it was gambling. Initially, when I was asked to join, I said, "Nope, I'm not doing it. What if I don't get to the middle of the circle? I wouldn't get any money, and I just wasted $25 or whatever." Plus, I learned my lesson about making honest money from the time I got scammed. That's a whole other story for a whole other day —just know I'll never make that mistake again.

Anyway, this was a little different to me, since I was only

contributing $25, and that was the most I could lose. Long story short, I eventually got into the position to make my money back, but I was tired of trying to recruit people and I was over the whole process. I told my friends that I was in that position, but I was tired of doing it. They laughed, and we moved on with our lives.

A few months later, May of 2020, a message was sent in a group thread that we have on Instagram regarding making easy money by scamming. After being burned a couple of times, I settled on the idea that God doesn't bless dirt; He blesses obedience and hard work. I sent the message, "I'll have to do a hard pass, you guys. God don't bless dirt." You would've thought that I said everybody who participates is going to hell. They brought up my involvement in the circle game, and the time I got scammed, and it just went from there.

I didn't get defensive, I just got irritated. I got irritated with the fact that I gave them a reason to think of me in that way, to think of me as a hypocrite. I'm sitting over here telling them that God doesn't bless dirt, but I was just trying to acquire easy cash a few months prior. The difference between my friends and I is the relationship we have with God and our level of knowledge regarding His word. I knew that we all have lessons to learn. I knew that if we all went through life perfectly, we would have no wisdom. I knew that in order to stand tall, you have to be knocked down a few times. At the end of the day, I grew from every mistake. My faith in God grew from every mistake because He was always there to protect me from my mess. My wisdom has grown from every learned lesson.

I realized then that not everyone will understand that. Not everyone will receive it, all I can do is plant the seed. It's God's job to water it, not mine. This poem was written during the exchanges I was having with my friends. You can see the frustration and the disappointment that I felt, not only with myself, but also with them. Don't ever let someone make you feel like you have to be perfect because you love Jesus. Strive to be the best you can be, but don't beat yourself up over a mistake. Learn from it, apply and live by the wisdom you gain from it, and try to be a positive example for others.

I Don't Mean to Boast

Year 2018

Others only see what I allow them to see.

I show them the kind and gentle, soft-spirited me.

I portray the morally-sound and integral side that makes the right choices all of the time.

I leak the goofy side that forgives everyone and releases grudges as soon as possible.

I demonstrate how a woman is supposed to carry herself.

A change in my environment doesn't cause a change in my character.

I pageant my beauty without being vain and narcissistic.

I exhibit mutual feelings of friendship and am not ashamed of with whom I begin to associate.

I allowed you all to bear witness to my epicness, my brilliance, my valor and my victory.

We were all made wonderfully different, but it was my God-given gift to be so set apart.

There is a reason I do not cry so easily,

Even though I want to burst into tears more often than not.

There is a reason you don't know my inner demons or the intimacy of my sexuality.

There is a reason I choose to barricade the malefic words that push to pry through my lips.

There is rationale behind my actions and my decisions so that I can avoid being hurtful.

You don't get to see the side of me that is angry, tempestuous, and blazing hot.

You probably didn't even know it existed.

You don't get to feel the bruises and the scars and the stitch-ridden palette of my beige flesh,

Left behind from past and present tongues of swords.

You didn't get to embark on the journey I've been on, but I'm open to share the

celebrations of my success.
My 180 degree turn ordered and placed my divine, beautiful, strong, and competent steps.
My heart is potent, strengthened by priceless pearls and sashes of ruby.
My light shone so bright in the sky, God told me well done.
I allow myself to be a piece of clay, molded by every experience and every obstacle I
encounter every time I rise in the morning.
In the years to come, I'm going to become a beautifully crafted pot,
being filled with everything

nice.

"In the years to come, I'm going to become a beautifully crafted pot, being filled with everything nice." I have not always accepted my calling from Christ. It took a while for me to come to grips with myself and truly receive His calling over my life. Matter of fact, I've only just recently accepted it. This poem was written well before my tug-of-war with God. This was also an assignment in high school. In my senior English class, we were studying epics, and our assignment was to write an epic boast. I don't like talking about my accomplishments unless I have to, and if I did, it would be for the sole purpose of job or scholarship opportunities. So for my epic boast, I left out all of my accomplishments, because that's not where my pride is placed. What I'm the most proud of is something that has no statistical evidence. I would rather talk about what I possess on the inside and what I have to offer morally, than talk about what I have accomplished in life. I feel like that's more of a flex anyway.

In this poem, I tried to focus on both my strengths and my weaknesses. My polished attributes as well as a few of my rough edges. A boast is not just about what you are good at and what you have done, but also what you need to improve on and better about yourself. If you are mature enough to acknowledge your flaws, that is a boast. Not everyone has achieved that level of maturity. I'm not saying I'm just the most mature person ever, but I don't shy away from admitting my faults, and to me, that's epic.

My objective in life has always been uncertain for me. I had no clue what I wanted to do and why I wanted to do it. One thing that I knew for sure was that I wanted to be a mother. That was the only thing set in stone. I didn't know what career path I wanted to take, I didn't know what I was most passionate about, I didn't even know the lifestyle I preferred.

During my journey, I studied the Bible. God told me to start with the book of Romans and then continue on to Matthew. Studying these books changed the trajectory of my mindset. I realized my sole purpose on this earth is to glorify God and to be His evangelist. I had to be faithful, shameless, hopeful, and fearless. It took a couple of months for me to fully surrender to this notion, but once I did, I turned into that "beautifully crafted pot." I felt my spirit shift, I literally felt a change in my soul. I am an instrument. I don’t mean to boast, but in the years to come, God is going to fill me “with everything nice.” I can’t wait.

Many People Are Like Seasons

Year 2020

Many people, like seasons,
Come and go.
The umbrella in the rain,
The plow through the snow.
God's purpose for them either
Temporary or permanent,
The hardest part is discerning the difference.
With the people you've grown to love
It's hardest to accept and it's not so obvious.
You plead your case to the sky and
Shout, "But I love them!"
But what does love have to do with the ending of a season?
I love warmth,
But still snow falls.
The wolves love the moon,
But the sun follows their calls.
You can try, but you'll fail,
If your plan is to plant an oak tree in a pot.
The roots will bust that clay that's frail,
Escaping the obstacle that's containing the lot.
So plant your oak in the soil of the ground,
Let its roots be free to grow.
The stronger its roots,

The more stable it'll be.

And despite the seasons that come and go,

Not one will move that tree.

Life is lived in seasons. Relationships exist and grow in seasons. Goals are accomplished in seasons. Hardships come in seasons. I've had many seasonal shifts in my life, and I'm only 19.

I had a friend who meant the world to me. She was —and is still — like my second sister. We were best friends for 13 years. She was by my side through every struggle I had with my confidence and the change I was experiencing during my transfer season. I was comfortable with telling her everything, and she was comfortable telling me everything. As we started to get older, the relationship was becoming unequally yoked.

She was drifting farther and farther away into left field. I began to worry for her safety. She pulled away in fear that I would tell her parents about what she was doing. For a moment, I seriously did consider hinting to her parents that she was purposely putting herself in harm's way. I didn't feel like it was my place to air out her dirty laundry, but if I had to choose between my friendship with her and her safety, I would choose her safety every time. I decided that I would rather just talk to her and see where her head was at, why she was doing what she was doing. I wanted to encourage her to find a different path, remind her that people genuinely love her, and point out to her that the people she was running with didn't have her best interest at heart.

As we spoke, the conversation began to sound stupider and stupider. No, stupider isn't a word, but by now you should've caught on to the fact that I have my own dictionary. I think she began to realize from the look on my face that I didn't buy into what she was saying, so then she just started crying. She apologized over and over again and cried on my shoulder. She told me how much she loved and appreciated me, how I was right, and that she would stop doing what she was doing. I heard her, and everything sounded all good, but I knew in my heart that it was nothing but talk. When she pulled away and I got to look in her face, I didn't recognize her. I didn't see the shine and light in her eyes. Someone who I had known for 13 years, I couldn't recognize by face. I knew from that point on, that her season in my life was complete, and I thank God for her in every prayer.

I have a friend whom I chose the minute I met her. People don't know this, but I have a hidden talent. I can literally walk into a room and choose the people I want to be friends with, and nine times out of ten, it comes to pass. True story. I walked into the room the second day of class of my junior year of high school, and I sat down. The roll was called, and I heard a name I recognized. I never saw the girl before, but I'd heard the name and was curious to see what she looked like. So, I turned around and looked, and immediately thought, *Oh wow she's cute. She looks like a senior*. Then I turned back around and minded my business for a good two weeks. Eventually, we became table-mates, and that's when I chose her to be my friend. She said something funny, and she was locked in. I'm just letting everyone know who's reading right now, that it is so easy to become my friend. Like, not a challenge at all. As long as you aren't a bully, and you love Jesus, welcome to the party.

She and I got closer and closer as the year progressed, and we became good friends. As the new friendship grew, we were simultaneously growing distant from our own best friends. She played a key role in my remaining high school years. She helped me build self-confidence and encouraged me to be unafraid to voice my opinion. She influenced some of the ways I dressed and some of the music I listened to, and I loved her company. She is absolutely hilarious, and she comes from a good family. When I graduated high school, she was going into her senior year. I am a year older than her. Of course, after not seeing each other every day and being forced to formulate new friendships, we also began to grow apart. We still remained close, but we weren't each other's "first" anymore —first for an outing, first for a vent session, first for good news, first for bad news, first for change in our lives, first for pretty much anything. It hadn't been that way before, but her season in my life was beginning to end, and I recognized that. There was no bad blood between us, no hidden issues, that I'm aware of. We simply grew apart. We remain close friends, but the season where she was my best friend is over, and sadly, the season of association is among us. She will always be my girl!

When I graduated high school, I couldn't wait to start working. Toward the end of the summer of 2019, August third to be exact, I got a job at the Forever 21 in the mall as a sales associate. (I will never forget that date because it was tax-free weekend and my first day of work …

trifling.)The girl I got my application from, was the same girl I turned my application back in to, and she was so dry. She didn't smile at me, she barely looked at me, and her voice was unpleasant. I'm pretty sure I saw her roll her eyes a few times. I just brushed it off and said whatever! But if she was going to be my future coworker, I had to be nice to her in spite of her demeanor toward me, so that she would see I was friendly. I care about what others think of me in the sense of reputation and character, and I wanted to start out on the right foot.

Fast-forward a little bit: I got the job and soon realized that this girl didn't talk much. She was nice to me when she was helping me at the cash register, but every time I said something, she would purse her lips and look at me like I had boo-boo on my face. She made me feel so slow. Every time she spoke to me, it was to correct me, and my face would show my embarrassment by blushing pink. As time went on, we got closer and closer. It turns out, she only talks to people she likes. For some reason, I felt a sense of loyalty to her, and I didn't know why. We basically just met. I just knew I would do anything for her. Anything she asked, I would do or try my best to do it. Anything she needed, I would try my best to provide.

The day that broke the ice was the day she rode with me to the bank. She didn't have any reason to go other than me asking her to. This was the first time I got to see her in an element other than work. She even bought me a dog-gone ice cream cone! I absolutely love ice cream. That's how I knew she was a keeper. I told y'all it's easy to be my friend. After that day, we started going on other outings, and we had great conversations. Sometimes, we would sit and talk for hours. She is spiritual and intelligent, and I love listening to intelligent people speak.

We would talk about God sometimes. I told her about my experience with God when I was in high school. We became more and more open and vulnerable with each other because of the trust we established in our long conversations. I truly believe God placed her in my life for growth. I have been able to learn more about myself and learn to respect other people's perspectives and opinions. God used her as an instrument to rebuild my relationship with Him. He gave me visions and dreams that I was supposed to share with her, that were about her! So, while God was speaking to me and revealing that He was still present in my life, He was simultaneously showing her that He was thinking of her and was working in her life as well. I had a lot of spiritual insecurities that I didn't realize. Insecurities like being afraid to admit when God was working in me, or being skeptical of the visions and dreams I was having, unsure whether it was really God or just my own imagination. Over time, I came to realize that it was, in fact, God.

Fast forward again, I got meningitis in March of 2020. March 13, to be exact. That is another day I will never forget. I had a 103-degree fever and pains so sharp in my head, that I thought I was having recurring seizures. That night I had a dream. The dream was about her. We were driving around in the middle of the night on Fair Park Boulevard close to downtown Little Rock. I knew it was Fair Park, but it didn't look like Fair Park. Instead of there being regular businesses, every block had a bank. The banks didn't have names, they were just all blue and lit up. We would stop at these banks, she would hold the door open for me, and inside of the bank would be an ATM. I would go to the ATM and make a withdrawal and a deposit, and then we would leave and go to the next bank. Then, all of a sudden, we were driving and talking. I don't remember the exact conversation, but it had something to do with our destination. Then, the scene shifted again, and we are standing in the middle of a desolate valley. There was a chain-link fence that enclosed us sitting up on top of the hills. We started having a conversation, and in the dream I was sick. I told her I couldn't hug her because I was sick, so I gave her a fist bump instead. I don't remember the exact details of the conversation, but I remember that the gist of it was me telling her that she let people hurt her too easily. She gave people too much space to hurt her, too many chances to hurt her. I remember grabbing her bowed down head in one hand, wiping her tears away, and smiling at her. I looked up on top of the hill and saw people waiting for me. People in trucks. One truck had several people, and the other truck had one. I looked to the side of me and saw that we were standing by an opening in the fence. It was the only opening. I remember telling her that I had to go, and I walked through the opening toward the top of the hill. When I looked back, I saw that she didn't follow me out of the fence. I wanted her to follow so badly, but she didn't. Then, the dream ended.

As soon as I woke up, God told me to call her and tell her what I saw. It was like 2:00 AM, and I was battling with God, saying, "She's probably not even awake." With every ring of the phone, I told myself I would hang up. Then she answered, and I was speechless. I cut right to the chase. I told her about the dream and what I saw. At the time I could remember exactly what I said to her moments before walking out of the fence, so I told her that. After I told her the dream, she was quiet. I asked her if she knew anything about what I was saying, and if she understood what I was talking about. She said she did.

In the weeks that followed, I tried to interpret my dream. I had no idea what God was trying to show me. I came to the conclusion that me walking out of that fence alone signified that I would have to distance myself from her and our friendship. That day, I wrote this poem. I was begging God to show me the truth because I didn't want to accept that one. Eventually, He did show me the truth, and it wasn't anywhere close to what I had thought. In fact, it had nothing to do with me, but everything to do with her and her situation. Again, God used me as an instrument to do His work, and I was so awestruck at His brilliance. I hope that it is in God's will for her season to be evergreen.

I've come to realize that God is trying to groom me into something sturdy. Like a clay pot going into a kiln, I came out of fire and was alchemized into something beautiful. I prayed to be used as an instrument, and here He is playing every note to perfection. I prayed for revelation, and here He is revealing every good and bad thing to me without a filter. He made me strong and independent, where before, I was dependent on the relationships I had with others for my self-worth and approval.

He helped me realize that if I wanted to grow in His Word and in the calling that He predestined for me, I would need to plant my seed in good soil. I am rooted in faith, rooted in the fruits of the spirit, a firm believer, and shameless in my walk. Many people, like seasons, come and go, and you can't let every winter destroy you. "So plant your oak in the soil of the ground, and let its roots be free to grow. The stronger its roots, the more stable it'll be, and despite the seasons that come and go, not one will move that tree."

To Be Seen

Year 2018

Cast a shadow over my face to create mystery behind my being.
Then I'll walk into a room, long strides in a step, daring to be seen.
The slight difference between attractive and attract-ability, don't downplay the meaning.
To breathe is to send out an invitation.
To act upon your will and to receive no condemnation.
To pursue the promise without hesitation.
To jump and to leap without knowing the destination.
You are not like me.
You think before you speak, but just barely.
I try to be sleek, but just can't be.
And you are constantly reminding, yourself and me,
That you are untouchable.
How does it feel to not be touched?
Untouched, yet stained with fingerprints.
Your face plastered upon one's eyes like a contact lens.
Your simple conversation leaves a stamp of your presence.
You are not like me!
You don't have to try to be seen,
You just are.

Light Skin Problems

Year 2017

I'm fair. I'm not white.
Don't deny me of my black,
Because it's there, it's just light.
And don't deny me of my culture,
Because I've lived it, it's my life.
Saying that "I don't understand" because of my skin
Is stereotypical, and it's a lie.
I'm not boujee, I'm not rich, and I'm smart
Because I do my work.
I'm not ghetto, I'm not ratchet, and my chest doesn't fill my shirt,
But am I any less black because my butt doesn't fill my skirt?
Am I any less black because my hips don't have a defined curve?
I have big legs, big arms, broad shoulders and thick lips.
My black is not defined by the protrusion of my hips.
My black is not defined by the state of my hair.
My black is not defined by the types of clothes I choose to wear.
Light skin, brown skin, dark skin, what's the difference?
All in the same boat, they didn't and don't care about complexion.
There's a "B" on that resumé,
There's a "B" on that application.
We separate ourselves, it's self-discrimination.
There are no separate teams, we're in this together.
So stop saying,

“It’s a light skin problem,”
It’s a black people problem.
“You’re not even black,”
What’s that supposed to mean?
Ignorance is a disease and it’s spreading quickly, so I repeat:
I’m fair. I’m not white.
And don’t deny me of my black,
Because it’s there.
It’s just light.

In society, we have this phenomenon called colorism. It is prejudice or discrimination against individuals with a dark skin tone, typically among people of the same ethnic or racial group. It is very present among the black community. We discriminate and judge amongst ourselves based on stigmas formulated by lack of exposure.

Even as a light-skinned woman, I get judged all of the time. I get told that I don't understand the struggle of black people. I get denied my experiences and my culture. I am told that I'm not really black, and so on. It used to, and still does, offend me… some of the things that my own people would say to me and about me. However, I am not so naive to admit that the tone my skin rids a certain level of hate from me that is experienced by other people. In the world, I am more widely accepted and deemed more beautiful, smart, safe, and more capable because of my lighter complexion. This is true for every ethnicity across the board (other than white people, who get spray tans, lay in tanning beds, and sit in the sun for hours on end to gain a little color. It's funny how they want our culture and characteristics, but would never really want to be black.)

Dark skin is so beautiful to me, and it's hard to believe that some people don't view it the same way. Of course, it stems from slavery. The slave owners would rape their slaves, have light babies, and would deem them more beautiful because they possessed European features. If the children were light enough, they would try to "pass" them for white and get them schooling, dress them nicely, and generally treat them with more respect and grace than they would their dark-complected counterparts. These wounds have transcended time, and the ideology remains because the stigma is still accepted as truth by white people. As a community, we need to take the time to understand each other's perspectives, lift each other up, and love on one another, because we are all that we have. No one else is going to do that for us.

One day, I sat down and wrote this poem as a testament to my blackness. I love being black. The beautiful thing about black people is that there is so much diversity within the race. We have so many different skin tones, body builds, hair types, textures and colors, languages and dialects, and so many other things that make us special. This poem is nothing less than a proud black woman announcing to her community that she would not be deemed less of a black person because of the tone of her skin.

Faith

Year 2020

Through your pain
I cry my tears.
I want to help you
Calm all of your fears.
Your voice is
A whistle in the wind.
Your thoughts are
A rash on my skin.
I itch to know
How you really feel.
I want to help you
But your lips are sealed.
Maybe it's not the right time,
Maybe I should wait until you come to me.
But I know I was sent for you,
And it's you I see.
You aren't invisible,
You will never be.
I know you better
Than I know myself.
And surprisingly
You know me.

I want to wipe your tears away.
I want to hold your cheeks in my hands.
I want to pray with you.
I want you to know where I stand.
Don't abandon your soul.
Don't isolate your heart.
Don't confine your mind.
Always listen before you start.
Hear His voice when you begin.
Listen to the Spirit speak.
I hate to see you suffering
Just let me in.
Let me do
What God assigned me to be for you.
He told me it'll be hard to get through,
But this is what I require of you.
That's why when I see you in distress
I do my best to uplift your mood.
I have a vested interest in your mental,
In my heart you have a room.
If you ever have to question
Who is there for you,
First think of God

And then think of me, too.

God heard my cry for a friend, someone who was spiritual like me. Someone who I could talk to and who would understand how I feel, and take it just as seriously as I do. Someone who could offer me advice that lined up with my ideology and wasn't contrary to my faith. I met her at my job. We are completely opposite of each other in more ways than not, so we are able to learn things about ourselves that we may not have known before, and also learn new perspectives.

She seemed to not value herself as much as I valued her. She didn't always see her power, and I tried to remind her every chance I got. She seemed to be going through some rough patches. She would be extra moody and would take everything personally. I would do my best to make her happy, and it would work temporarily. I hated to see her down. I wanted her to know that if there was anything she needed, I would be more than happy to be the one to provide it, whether it was advice or just a listening ear. Her name is Faith, and this poem is named after her.

No Control

Year 2019

It doesn't matter how much you love me.
It doesn't matter how much you care.
You spit fire through your teeth,
And leave traces of shit in your hair.
You make promises you don't keep,
Making life even more unfair.
What I see is disappointing, and my heart is slowly starting to tear.
What a beautiful face with so much promise,
Has enough confidence to spare.
Lacks discipline and self-control,

Oh what a terrible pair.

You know what's jacked up? When someone you love starts changing for the worst right in front of your eyes, and you know you can’t do anything about it. That hurts. I lost my best friend of 13 years just like this. We had been friends since I was about five years old, and it lasted until I was 17. She was like a sister to me. We told each other everything in confidence, we challenged each other, and we had a ton of fun all of the time.

As we got older, our values began to differ in extreme ways. She started purposely putting herself in harm's way. She hung out with people who were involved in the wrong things, jumped into a gang, started scamming, and other things that she didn’t have any business doing. The thing is, we were both raised in the church, knowing right from wrong. She still knew right from wrong, she just chose to disregard it and try to be someone she wasn’t.

I could see the early signs of this when she used to lie about her age when we were younger. When she would lie to her parents about places we had been and what we were doing there, even though it wasn’t anything to lie about to begin with. Little things that I didn’t treat as a “big deal,” because they really weren't at the time. I thought, *That's just her; it's just how she is*. This poem was inspired by the changes I was beginning to see in my friend and our relationship.

Angel on Earth

Year 2020

Emotions flood over me
Like a river beaks a dam.
Built over time,
This pressure of mine.
Why can't I feel it instead.
Why do I block the thoughts inside my head?
Afraid to let it out,
Afraid someone will hear me.
Hold my vulnerability so close to my heart,
But it has a lethal ability.
Stabbing every inch of me,
My soul feels empty.
Piecing people together to get a greater picture.
I know even though I don't see it,
My God is with her.
The path isn't straight,
It's long and windy.
Life isn't easy.
Angels deserted on earth
To complete a deed unknown.
Lonely hearts,
Forced to be strong.

I went through a phase in which I wanted to be an angel. Like, a legitimate angel. I wanted nothing more than to serve and glorify God, and what better way to do that than to be an angel? It made perfect sense to me. I would pray fervently asking God if He accepted angel applications. Did He even appoint new angels? How do you become an angel?

I watched videos on YouTube, surfed the internet, and eventually asked my father (who is a minister) if God appointed new angels and how I could be one. He explained to me that angels were God's workers, whose sole job is to serve Him and carry out His work. Angels never get to rest, angels don't have choices, angels were created solely for the purpose of servitude. In my mind, I was like, *Okay what's your point? Isn't that what God calls us to do as well?* He explained to me that yes, that is what God calls us to do here on earth and to acknowledge Him in all that we do, but we obtain the reward of rest whenever we pass away. When we pass, ideally, we have fulfilled the purpose God has for us, therefore our job is complete. Angels never complete a purpose; they are forever fulfilling it. Whenever I heard that, I received it and went back upstairs and immediately prayed to

God that I didn't want to be an angel anymore.

During this phase, I was searching for a spiritual partner. Someone I could comfortably talk to, and share everything I was feeling, and why I was feeling it —in confidence. I looked on my school campus, in my church, in my old friend groups, in my new friend groups, and even at work. I was searching for something that wasn't mine to search for. I was trying to piece together a bunch of different people to kind of formulate an ideal friendship. Almost like patchwork, I wanted to take the fun from this person, the kindness and generosity from that person, the wisdom from someone else, the spirituality from another, and the conversational aspects of someone else, and so on. I was putting so much weight into all of these different relationships, and ultimately giving them too much power over my happiness and control to dictate how I feel.

I was "piecing people together to get a greater picture." Instead of looking for God, I was looking for faith in people to pick me up when I was down, to comfort me when I was unsettled or worried, to give me joy, to give me advice, and to help me make the right decisions. I was subconsciously trying to replace God with people. In doing so, I became lonely, even though I was constantly surrounded by others. I put up a huge front, trying to look happy and fulfilled and blessed. I wanted to be a light for others, even though I was in complete darkness. “Lonely hearts, forced to be strong.”

I felt like a deserted angel on Earth.

So What, She's a Woman

Year 2018

She is a woman, so is She inferior?
She is capable of working just as hard as Her counterpart,
So what makes him the superior?
They attended the same classes, performed the same tasks,
Earned the same job, but don't acquire the same cash.
She is a woman, so is She weaker?
If She is so weak, then why is She sought after?
Physicality is but one aspect that She doesn't need to have,
This woman has a will and sharp thinking,
A dominant force, who doesn't need the "other half."
These men, they need Her optimism,
They need Her meticulous mind.
They want Her organized thought process, qualities in a man that are hard to find.
She chooses her battles wisely and knows that failure and success go together.
Persistence is key,
So She works hard and long, no matter the weather.
She is a woman, so is Her time less valuable to you?
That's what is conveyed when She is short-changed the pay that is due.
Taking care of Her family is Her concern,
She works too hard to not get what She earns.
Maybe She's the breadwinner between the two,
But She's still making a percentage less than Her man, I guarantee you.
If you don't believe me you can look up the facts, they'll be there.

I'm just here to make sure you're more aware.
When a problem doesn't affect you, you turn the other cheek,
Then all hell breaks loose when it decides to march down your street.
She wasn't created by accident, so She deserves to be treated equivalent.
Maybe if more people begin to think this way,
She will be able to reap Her benefits someday.

Count on Me

Year 2020

Man, I don't think I can count on anybody.
I can only count on myself to remember words not kept.
I count on myself to remember promises broken and the feeling I felt when my back was stabbed.
The feeling of betrayal and wrongful guilt.
I can count on the images flashing through my head,
Images of myself lying on the floor staring at the ceiling thinking,
Or the image of me crying in my pillow when I went to bed.
The feeling of knowing that I don't have anybody to go to when I have heaviness on my heart,
A heaviness that I'm almost ashamed of,
So heavy that if I tried to explain it,
I wouldn't know where to start.
I can't count on anyone to listen and understand exactly,
I can only count on myself to understand me.
I can only count on myself to be the person who knows all of my feelings.
The ones that show and the ones I'm even uncomfortable experiencing privately.
I can count on me praying for,
Smiling at,
Unconditionally loving,
And accepting me.
I don't think I can count on anybody,

Except God and myself.

There was a moment in my life where I felt completely alone. I felt there was no one I could turn to for reassurance, support or comfort. I felt like no one could understand all of the intricacies of my emotions. I had so much going on inside of my mind at the time, and I didn't do anything about it. Don't get me wrong, I wanted to, but the sad truth was that I was embarrassed with what I had to say and how I felt. Even if I did talk to someone, I wouldn't have known where to start. Do I start with being bullied in 7th grade? Do I start with the emotional trauma I experienced in 10th grade? Do I start with the insecurities I developed in 12th grade? Do I start with beginning college and doing things I told myself I would never do? Or do I start with how I was losing myself completely? None of those seemed to be good starting points, because none of those seemed like the beginning of the story.

All I knew at this point, was that I only had myself to count on. Myself and God.

Lust

Year 2020

You don't even have to move,
Just let me take you in.
I wanna know how you feel,
I want to touch your skin.
I want to feel your lips,
Warm on the nape of my neck
I want you to know how I taste,
And I want to absorb your flesh.
While we are here for a moment,
It feels like forever.
Complete in your presence,

To lust I surrender.

Something that I take pride in is my virginity. I am going on 20 years old and am still a virgin. Whenever I say this, sometimes people don't believe me, and I can understand why. Being a virgin nowadays is commendable, but not popular. For some reason, I don't feel like I'm missing anything. I have no desire to have sex. My body reacts to certain things, sure, I'm human. However, the desire isn't really there.

God tells me that my body is a temple. God also says in His Word that intercourse should be between a man and his wife. Not his girlfriend, fiancé, friend with benefits, boyfriend, or whatever else. Same for women. I try to live my life as pleasing to God as possible. There are a lot of things I can't control in my life, but what I do to and with my body is completely my choice. What helps me the most is remembering that my life and body is not my own, I belong to God. I want to give Him my best effort and to try my best to be obedient. Even though I try to live according to His Word, I still have my own cross to bear —controlling my temper.

I know my view is unpopular, especially among most of my friends. I try not to engage in conversations about the topic because I know that I can't contribute much, other than to be safe about it. This poem is just showing a more relatable side of me. I am normal. Sometimes I want some of the same things everybody else wants and desires! However, I made a promise to God and a promise to myself, that I would wait to have sex until marriage.

The Gift of Lesson

Year 2018

“Respect yourself,” she says.
No one will respect you as much as you will.

“Value your body and your time,” she says.
Not everyone is worth the sacrifice.

“You are beautiful and smart,” she says.
Your opinion matters just as much as anyone else’s.

“Don’t get caught up in what everyone else is doing,” she says.
You’re not everyone else.

“Don’t be a sucker to the world,” she says.
Temptation is real, but so is integrity.

“Don’t be afraid to ask questions,” she says.
If you aren’t learning something new every day, that’s a problem.

“Filter what you feed into your body,” she says.
Both physically and spiritually.

“Dare to be different,”

“Shoot for the stars,” she says.

“You can achieve anything you put your mind to,”

"I'm doing this because I love you."
"Take pride in what you do," she says.
The little things matter too.

"Be a friend to the friendless,"
"Be an example for others to be able to follow," she says.
A beacon of light in a dark room.

My mother said these things to help me better myself, that's why I say the same to you.

Like many can attest, my mother is the most influential person in my life. Everything good about me, I learned from her —kindness, respectfulness, thoughtfulness, everything. She has a heart of gold, and the one word I would use to describe her is *jolly*. She's just happy all of the time unless otherwise provoked. To me, that's the most admirable trait she possesses. She can lift anyone's mood, she always knows what to say and how to say it, she's "comfort" in human form. She has always encouraged my siblings and me to be the best version of ourselves, whatever that looks like.

I am like a sponge when it comes to advice. I hear it, receive it, accept it, and try my best to apply it to my life. My mother gives the absolute best advice. This poem is just the tip of the iceberg for some of the guidance she gives me. I remember when I felt like I had to be somebody different to be accepted. I wanted nothing more than to fit in with the people I was surrounded by, nothing more than to adapt to my environment and morph into my surroundings. I felt like this was the only way I was going to be seen. In the midst of the identity crisis that I was going through, my mother dropped a gem of advice —the affirmation I needed to hear to save myself from total personality and character dissipation.

She said, "You are enough. You don't have to change for people to like you; people love you just the way you are." It seems so simple, but this was an eye-opener for me. I never felt like I was enough. I never felt like people would like me if I allowed myself to be quirky and awkward, or deep and spiritual, or goofy and soft, all at the same time. All of these insecurities that I didn't even know I possessed, flooded over me when she said those words. I started crying, because I thought, *If other people can accept me, why can't I accept myself?*

After years of reflection and growth, trial and error, and testing the waters, I finally became unapologetically me. I embraced everything I had to offer, and guess what: people love me more than they did before.

Thank you momma for not letting me give in to myself. Thank you for always being my listening ear and the voice of reason when I was being unreasonable. Thank you for being a perfectly imperfect model for Kendal and I. I cannot thank you enough for the lessons you have taught me. They are the greatest gifts you could ever give me, and I will cherish them and pass them on to anyone who has ears to hear. I love you.

I'm Beat

Year 2019

I want to be in love,
Really, I do.
But how am I supposed to when my heart keeps breaking in two?
When I open the doors, the floodgates come through,
Emotions rattle my brain and my heart beats for you.
When I look in your face, I don't feel special.
I don't feel good enough, I don't feel the potential.
No kindling fire, no heat or desire.
Just heartbreak when I see you beside HER.
Supposed to be my guy.
Laughing under the light of pearls.
Now you're asking for my advice on how to get with some other girl.

Changes

Year 2019

Have you ever considered how quickly your life can change?
There's always that not-a-part-of-the-plan circumstance that
stops you in your tracks.
And people start asking you, “What's next?"
Well, you can take a guess,
be my guest,
while I'm over here trying to figure out the rest without your pessimistic
opinion corrupting my thought process.
I refuse to let negativity disrupt my positive progress,
and can I just be honest...
Prayer is holding everything together,
like holy mud in a secular birds nest.
And expectations built up over time only make me hope I can meet
what you expect, better yet,
exceed what you expect of me.
Overflow over the cracked porcelain rim with money...
No, with happiness.
I desire to be much more than rich,
I long to be fulfilled.

And when I accomplish this not-so-crazy pitch,
The oceans will be still,
the trees will have to kneel,
the clouds will have to part,
gifting the sun's warmth I will feel,
running through my body like my blood is the track,
and my bones are the field.
I've turned into an activity fiend.
Never at the house because I don't want to miss anything.
The constant swipe down to refresh,
I'm too worried about what other people are doing.
Procrastinating on every single priority
because my face is lost in a screen.
So I steal some time out of the week
to unwind and only worry about me and
what I got going.
Please,
Tell me.
Have you ever wondered how quickly your life can change?
Believe me, it's not subtle,
The difference is black and white.

It's like yesterday leads into tomorrow night with no time in between.

Be careful not to live your life fearfully.

Nothing paralyzes like yielding to fear.

However, nothing vitalizes courage like faith,

so live your days faithfully.

Not only on the good ones when everything goes your way,

But on the bad days especially.

Be careful not to blink because you'll miss everything.

Have you ever considered how quickly your life can change?

You wake up in the morning without a care in the world,

Completely worry-free,

you go play outside and pick every flower that your mother says are weeds,

everywhere you go,

others cater to your needs,

everything is peachy when you're four or below feet.

Then you go to sleep.

And you wake up with bills to pay,

Nothing to eat,

And a quarter of a tank of gas to get you from

Point A to point B.

Do you see how quickly...?

From my point of view,
I have peace.
I know that my roots run deep and that God
Has a plan for me as long as this blood runs warm through my veins.
He's blessed me with beauty,
An able body,
and intelligence pulsing through my brain.
I have no excuse to be caught up on yesterday,
Unless to today it pertains.
He did not create me to follow others unless it's wisdom I will gain.
And I will forever proudly let my light so shine
Through the shade like a
White shirt with a red Kool-aid stain.
I'm trying my best to fulfill what God created me to be.
You can call me whatever names:
Extra, goody-goody or lame.
But I am a witness to how quickly life can change.
It can be swept from under your feet without you
Realizing or ever knowing,
So everything good that I see,

I want to experience it personally.
I live my life and dance my jig happily,
Not caring too much about who's watching.
I've learned that I won't always be comfortable,
I've gotten used to sitting uncomfortably.
If I take time for myself,
That doesn't mean I'm acting selfishly,
But in order to be there for those who need me,
I have to be mentally,
Physically,
And spiritually healthy.
And because of this,
I can say I'm proud of myself for
Acknowledging the changes respectfully.
Acknowledgment is a gift,
It encourages dignity, all the while inviting humility,
And once you inherit these qualities,
You will not take for granted another day,
And you will be ready for how quickly
Life can change.

Overstayed My Welcome

Year 2020

What’s the point of speaking, when no one wants to hear my voice.
I feel like I’ve overstayed my welcome,
I’ve overstepped my boundaries.
I’ve spoken up too much about things that don’t matter to anyone but me,
And now what matters most gets overshadowed with the expectation of inappropriate voicing.
My opinion is blemished,
My passions dismissed,
My story silenced,
The experiences that lead to my vocalizing waved off as irrelevant.
I’m tired of speaking, so I’ll write instead.
Yelling and shouting my truth in my head.
There is no misconceiving there.
I know what I mean,
I know my intentions.
Instead of giving other people the power to discredit my being,

I’ll just stop speaking.

I am a very opinionated person. Sometimes this is received well; sometimes it's not. "I've spoken up too much about things that don't matter to anyone but me, and now what matters most gets overshadowed with the expectation of inappropriate voicing." I believe that the little things matter. I pay attention to them, I care about them, I speak up when they aren't paid attention to by anyone else. This is often seen as nit-picky and petty. My words are often misconceived because people expect me to mean something that I don't, or believe something that I won't, and all of a sudden the whole room is against me. I'm not a very open person and don't really let people into that more vulnerable side of me, so they have no idea why I feel what I feel. Then again, if I was asked I wouldn't mind sharing, but no one ever cares to ask me. They just like to get mad about the product that my mind presents.

One day, I said something so simple. My brother needed a haircut. I said, "Noah, you need a haircut," and then boom, attack. "WHY ARE YOU ALWAYS ATTACKING HIM?" I just sat there confused as to why my mother was making a big deal out of nothing. After sitting there listening and then trying to explain that I simply pointed out the obvious and meant no harm by it, I just stopped talking and made the decision to stop talking for the rest of my life unless I actually had something very important to say — which, might I add, is nearly impossible for me, and I wouldn't even be able to do it if my life depended on it. I would definitely die. However, when I made that promise to myself, I decided I would write everything down instead. That's when I wrote this poem. "Instead of giving other people the power to discredit my being, I'll just stop speaking."

I concluded that I was being unreasonable, and that what I was saying wasn't the problem, it was how frequently I said it. I decided that instead of pointing out the little things, I would just keep them to myself. I want it to be that when I speak, others know that it's important. It's really a win-win situation. I can mind my business in peace, and they can figure everything out themselves. Tee-hee.

In all seriousness, I had to come to grips with the idea that not all battles are worth fighting. I was tired of being shut down, so I decided to start picking and choosing where I spent my energy.

I've Been Trying

Year 2020

Jesus, I'm uncomfortable.
What is it that I need to be doing?
I act on what I think I'm hearing, trying to distinguish
Your voice and separate it from my own thoughts, I'm in need of the spirit of discerning.
Lord, I'm unsettled.
This unsettling feeling shaking and straddling the waist of my mind, like I'm made of pebbles.
Afraid to make one wrong move, or say one wrong thing, in fear of crumbling.
Jesus, I'm tired.
I'm tired of questions and guessing,
of trying and failing,
of starting and not finishing,
of speaking and not acting.
Just for once, I want to be proud of me.
My life feels like it's at a standstill, despite all of the things I'm doing.
I'm trying to listen, I've been trying.
I want to be obedient.
I want to give You all of me all of the time,
And then feelings of unworthiness start sneaking in.
Thoughts that linger, reminding me how unfit I am, surely resulting in my disqualification.
It seems like every day the struggle is the same, trying to please You and hear what You say,
and all that I have to cling to is

"Everything is going to be okay."
That constant reminder that rings in my head when the light turns to dark.
It makes me pick my chin up, and temporarily feel important in some way.
Driven by a newfound confidence,
desperate to express and prove my faith by acting in obedience.
Prove my relationship by praying out loud and expecting a reply.
Prove that I have joy,
prove that I'm growing,
prove that I love You,
prove that I'm sowing,
prove everything I possibly can,
more to myself than to You,
That I really am trying.
But You hear my silent cries, and You feel the weight of my heart.
You see my deepest desires, and how I'm tearing myself apart.
In search of something so blatantly clear, if it was a snake it would bite me.
To know Him is one thing, to obey Him is a little more tricky.
My eyes feel veiled, my ears feel nailed closed.
Jesus, I'm trapped.
I stand here vulnerable and unclothed.
Lord, I need You right now to come bless my soul.
Awaken in me something new and refreshing.
Replenish the river that now runs dry.
Raise the head I once held high.
I'm trying to listen, and I've been trying.
Comfort me and settle my heart.

Relieve the fatigue of my spirit, award me yet another fresh start.

I offer myself over and over again,

And I will pray without ceasing.

As long as I shall live and even after then,

I won’t stop believing that

You believe in me.

The day God spoke to me, I was smack-dab in the middle of my first depression. I was on the floor crying for seemingly no reason on a Sunday morning. The radio was playing gospel music and the Rickey Smiley Morning Show provided the Sunday gossip. I remember waking up sad. I got ready quietly and emotionless. Then, when I got to the bathroom, I couldn't even look at myself. I started crying softly, and then it got harder and harder to stand. My knees buckled and I sat on my bathroom floor, ready to give up, ready to accept defeat, ready to succumb to darkness.

I stopped crying when I heard something familiar. I realized that the radio had just said my name. I thought I heard wrong, so I listened to see if it would repeat it. Rickey Smiley was talking, and sure enough, he said it again. He said, "Nyah? I don't know what's going on right now in your life, but God told me to tell you that everything is going to be okay." He said it twice. My jaw dropped, and I let my mouth hang wide open. He said some other encouraging things, and then it went to a commercial break. I can't remember what else he said because I had heard all I needed to hear. All of a sudden, there was an indescribable peace that settled over me, warm like a blanket. I immediately wiped my tears away and smiled. I looked up as if I could see God himself, and I imagined Him smiling right back at me. He reminded me who and Whose I was. He reminded me that He would never leave, nor forsake me.

Present-day, and I'm still clinging to that promise that He made to me five or so years ago. I don't worry about my future because I know I am highly favored and have already been told I'm going to be alright. However, just because I knew everything would work for the good and would turn out okay in the end, it didn't mean that I wasn't lost. Just a couple of months ago, which was like April 2020, I wanted nothing more than to know my purpose and my gifts. I wanted so desperately to start my purpose in Christ and to help others on their journeys.

"It seems like every day the struggle is the same, trying to please You and hear what You say, and all that I have to cling to is "Everything is going to be okay."' There was an inexplicable discomfort and unsettling in my spirit. I prayed fervently and pleaded with God to show me in any way He deemed necessary, what it was that I was supposed to be doing, where I was supposed to be doing it, and who I was supposed to be doing it with. I prayed with no success. I had no clue about anything. Around this time, I started getting into the habit of watching interviews of admirable people. I watched interviews with people like DeVon Franklin and Meagan Good-Franklin, Issa Rae, Yvonne Orji, and others who I felt had something valuable to say, and could help me understand a bit more about myself. My spirit was fed by the Franklins; I tapped into my gift of literary creativity by listening to Issa; and I was reminded by Yvonne that you can be a boss chick and still love Jesus and respect yourself. I absolutely love listening to intelligent people speak. After I had watched the interviews, I would re-watch them and pause the video after the interviewer asked the question. I would answer the question myself, like I was the one being interviewed. Listening to these individuals fueled my spirit and made me beg God more and more to simply give me a HINT at this point!

Then, one day it just hit me. I like to write, I'm good at it, my gift is writing and that's the path God wants me to take. After weeks of countless ideas and brainstorms, my mind was all over the place. I started a podcast that never saw the light of day, and then I started a book that was based off of the podcast that didn't get past the first chapter. Then I wanted to write a movie script, then I wanted to write another book about the funny moments in my life, and then I wanted to write a television series script, and it was just a lot going on 'in the membrane.'

I believe that during that time of confusion, God was just giving me an opportunity to practice discernment. Based on what I knew to be true —I was great at writing and English —and what I was trying to figure out —my God-given gift —everything just clicked. After it clicked and I decided to put my poems in a book, it's like God congratulated me for finally listening. My spirit was settled. I was no longer uncomplacent. I had tried to listen, and I had been trying. I finally heard Him, and He has been opening doors ever since.

I went to my special spot one day, a spot that God led me to. I went there when I needed to feel God directly, when I needed to speak out loud and connect with His creation. When I went back there, after I had finished half of the book, I decided to dedicate the book to Him. I brought the makeshift book I had put together with all of my poems inside, and I read them all aloud into the air. I was giving His words back to Him, for Him to do as He pleased with them. When I was finished, I looked up at the sky and smiled again, imagining that He was smiling right back at me. I knew everything was going to be fine. “As long as I shall live, and even after then, I won’t stop believing that You believe in me.”

This poem airs out all of my spiritual insecurities and every negative thought that I was feeling at the time. How could God use someone who was the least qualified? Nobody knows who I am, no one knows my name! How was I supposed to do this great work for all to see? How was He going to use me and I’m only nineteen? That’s really how I felt. I felt unworthy, and I felt that there were so many other people who were better qualified. I was honest and transparent with God, but at the same time I was inviting Him in to fulfill any purpose He saw fit, no matter how I felt about it. I learned that God doesn’t appoint the qualified, he anoints the available. As soon as you surrender to God your life and your gifts to use as He pleases, you’ll be amazed at the wonders He does.

Victory Lap

The word "manifest" seems like it just hit the mainstream media's vocabulary list. It's all over twitter, viral instagram posts, facebook posts, etc. Everybody is saying it. The word has been around forever, but you know how the internet works.

I believe manifestation is real, but I think that the overuse of the term is starting to take a bit of the spirituality away. Everybody is wanting to speak and manifest things into existence for their future selves, but aren't doing the necessary things in order to truly prompt the manifestation.

God said in James 2:17, that faith without works is dead. This simply means that in order to truly manifest things into existence, you must have faith that God will grant your desires according to His will, and that you must meet Him halfway by doing everything in your power to work towards that goal. Prayer, faith and manifestation all go together. You cannot be successful in one without the others.

I called myself manifesting a lot of things, simply because people told me that's what I should do. People would say, "Just speak positivity and manifest it, and it will come to be," trying to be all deep. And while this was great advice, it was missing a very important tidbit: including complete faith and trust that God will handle what I cannot control. I would pray so hard and I would cry, but crying didn't get me anywhere but upset. Praying would just make me more and more frustrated. Not only with myself, but also with God. The whole time, God is looking down on me shaking His holy head like, *when is this girl going to get it?*

Long story short, I got it eventually and that's when this book came to be. To be honest, it is simultaneously one of the most fulfilling and stressful things I've done. I'm even starting to have eczema flare ups, and I've never had eczema before. I think it's just the thought of putting myself out there in the rawest form I've ever allowed. It's really crazy when I think about it. However, I trust God more than I trust myself. If He says this is what I need to do, then so be it. I can throw my feelings out of the window.

I was on DeVon Franklin's prayer instagram live earlier this week, June 30, 2020, and I wanted to be added in so badly. I wanted to tell him about everything that had happened since we last spoke. I wanted him to know that my book was almost ready to publish, I wanted to just share my excitement and ask that he pray for patience over my spirit! I didn't get picked, but I was fine with that. It would make it that much more special when I got to tell him that it was published!

As you can probably tell (or maybe not), this "Victory Lap" piece was created after all of the formal editing and proofreading. At this point, the manuscript has already been sent to be professionally proofread and I'm currently waiting on it to be returned to me. However, I felt that this piece should be included because it is the most current feeling that I am experiencing. I was initially going to leave off with "I've Been Trying" because the narrative was so telling, but when I wrote "Victory Lap", I just knew I was supposed to include it in the book.

I am astronomically far from the finish line. It's not over until it's over. However, "Victory Lap" is not only a triumphant poem, it is also a prophetic poem. It's inclusive of every little and large personal triumph. Triumphs over depression and insecurities. Triumphs over triggers and temperament, over shortcomings and failures, over drugs and disappointments. Triumphs over emptiness and discomfort, relationships and heartbreaks, anxiety and fear. Even after all of these victories along the way, I know that there is still a lot of work to be done.

God says to write out the vision and make it plain. I don't know everything, but I'm guessing this gives you goals that you can actually see and work towards —things that seem very tangible and simple. I'm guessing this would make it easier to stay on track and to keep from letting distractions veer you away from what God has for you. That's just my interpretation. With accordance to this statement, I did just that —I wrote out the vision plainly. I want to use my gifts. All of them. I want to be a best-selling author and a motivational speaker. I want to be an actor and a screenwriter for film and television. I want to be a journalist for Essence Magazine and I want to start my own podcast. None of these line up with my current reality or the reality that others expect me to have. That's fine. God already showed me snippets, so I don't really need any co-signs from anybody or even myself.

In God's perfect time, I will be what He has created me to be, and

I'll be able to take that victory lap, shouting praises and testimonies from the mountaintop.

Victory Lap
Year 2020

My life has meaning.

The time I spent shackled to my own being,

Searching for a wonder to quench my thirstiness,

Developing bruises on my knees from praying so fervently so frequently,

My life has purpose.

And every single bruise,

Welt,

Blood, sweat and tear stain

Was worth it.

Testimonies are nothing short of humility hearings.

How dare you think you unshackled yourself on your own!

I object the notion that you accomplished wonders alone!

I can see straight through you.

My life has favor,

And I'd be lying if I said I could tell you why.

God has a habit of appointing the most unqualified,

But I do know this:

Your willingness to be obedient, will carry you in strides.

And your faith, even in the most troubling of times, is pleasing to God.

Your life has meaning,

Your life serves a purpose.

Tend to your wounds,

Unshackle your feet.

Grow from the bruises and the beating.

See the wonders placed before you.

Your testimony is a testament of His grace.

The least you can do,

Is let your light shine through

So that when people look at you in your face,

They see God, too.

And to Him I reverent the highest praise.

Everything you see that is good in me—

Faithfulness, love, joy, kindness, and peace—

Is a reflection of God's instrumentation.

He plays every chord to perfection,

Every note has precision,

And every beat, intention.

So when you reflect back on your past afflictions,

And you recognize how God's sparing hand was in every situation,

Don't suppress the shout, or the song, or the dance, or the prayer, or the tears.

Shamelessly rejoice and give thanks,

Make the struggle worth it.

Go and take your victory lap,

God deserves it.

About the Book

Therapy comes in all shapes and forms. For me, it's poetry and journaling. "In Favor of Everything Right" compiles poems derived from my therapeutic sessions between God and I, and the context behind some poems in the form of a narrative. Also included are poems that were written about and inspired by the desires, weaknesses, and struggles of the flesh. Not everything that I have written is spiritual, but they all serve a purpose in God's will. Despite my fear of vulnerability, I —through growth and much communion with God —have realized the power and importance of testimony. This book tackles *depression*, *insecurities*, *relationships*, *spirituality*, and more. Real life people go through real life things, and being a Christian doesn't exempt you from the growing pains of life. Get ready to receive a gift given to you by God himself, because Lord knows I would never do this on my own terms!

I'm so excited to open my heart and mind to other people who might need some encouragement, reassurance, and the reminder that it is okay to be human. It's okay to not have your guard up and your mask on all of the time.

"If I alone bear witness about myself, my testimony is not deemed true." ***John 5:31***

"It is good for me that I was afflicted, that I might learn your statutes." ***Psalm 119:71***

Made in the USA
Coppell, TX
06 October 2020